兒童品格聖經

The CNV Kid's Bible: A Character Builder

New Testament Stories
新約故事
第三次印刷
Third Printing

兒童品格聖經——新譯本：新約篇
The CNV Kid's Bible:
A Character Builder-New Testament Stories

主　　　　編：黎永明
聖經故事作者：杜　嘉
品格故事作者：葉淑芳、張詠舒、鄭子遜
譯　　　　者：麥銘奇、鍾畢珊
編　　　　輯：陳少蘭、李淑婷、胡文芳
插 圖 設 計：麥志雄、趙樂琳
版 面 設 計：陳藹詩、楊明明、黃少卿

中文金句引自《聖經新譯本》，英文金句引自 The Holy Bible, English Standard Version
©2012　　　　環球聖經公會有限公司　　THE WORLDWIDE BIBLE SOCIETY LTD.
　　　　　　　版權所有　　　　　　　　All rights reserved
　　　　　　　初　版（2012年5月）　　1st Edition（May 2012）
　　　　　　　第三印（2013年3月）　　3rd Printing（March 2013）
　　　　　　　Cat. No.: BS1050　　　ISBN: 978-988-8124-36-7

環球聖經公會辦事處
香　港　　香港九龍土瓜灣貴州街6號東方報業大廈6字樓
　　　　　6/F, Oriental Daily News Building, 6 Kwei Chow Street, Tokwawan, Kowloon, Hong Kong
　　　　　Tel: (852) 2356 7234　　　Fax: (852) 2356 7389　　　E-mail: info@wwbible.org
新加坡　　221 Henderson Road, #02-02, Singapore, 159557
　　　　　Tel: (65) 6276 2981　　　Fax: (65) 6276 2980　　　E-mail: singapore@wwbible.org
台　灣　　台灣10074台北市羅斯福路1段24號2樓
　　　　　2F, No. 24, Section 1, Roosevelt Road, Jhongjheng District, Taipei City 10074, Taiwan
　　　　　Tel: (886-2) 2395 6191　　　Fax: (886-2) 2395 8137　　　E-mail: taiwan@wwbible.org
菲律賓　　c/o #13 Denver Street, Cubao, Quezon City, Philippines
　　　　　Tel: (63-917) 814 7223　　　Fax: (63-2) 410 0329　　　E-mail: philippines@wwbible.org
美　國　　10883-B South Blaney Avenue, Cupertino, CA 95014, USA
　　　　　Tel: (1-408) 996 8388　　　Fax: (1-408) 996 2838　　　E-mail: usa@wwbible.org
加拿大　　29 Brownell Street, Whitby, Ontario, L1R 0C6, Canada
東　岸　　Tel: (1-905) 903 7683
加拿大　　6560 Innsmoor Place, Burnaby B.C. V5E 4G3, Canada
西　岸　　Tel: (1-604) 307 8773　　　E-mail: canada@wwbible.org

網址：www.wwbible.org / www.wwbibleus.org

送給親愛的
THIS BIBLE BELONGS TO

丁劍雄
Nolan

你的　　袁姨媽
GIVEN BY　Auntie Dorothea

日期　　2014
DATE

場合
OCCASION

孩童個人資料
Personal Record

姓名...
Name

出生日期...
Date of Birth

父親姓名...
Father's Name

母親姓名...
Mother's Name

哥哥姓名...
Elder brother(s)' Name(s)

姊姊姓名...
Elder sister(s)' Name(s)

弟弟姓名...
Younger brother(s)' Name(s)

妹妹姓名...
Younger sister(s)' Name(s)

新約故事目錄
Table of Contents for New Testament Stories

品格塑造故事目錄
Table of Contents for Character Builder Stories

序 言
 給 家 長 的 話

　　神建立家庭，是要讓人在家裡享受地上最親密的人際關係，也讓父母可以在這個充滿愛的環境裡養兒育女。家長要子女學會待人處事的智慧，就應該從品格入手。究竟家長可以怎樣塑造子女的品格呢？《兒童品格聖經》專為3至9歲的孩童撰寫，又為家長勾畫出建構子女品格的藍圖，當中共有52個單元，每單元包括七個部份：1. 聖經故事；2. 背一背（金句）；3. 品格塑造（故事或見證）；4. 禱告；5. 想一想·做一做（反省問題）；6. 童來兒嬉（遊戲）；7. 家長提示。

　　《兒童品格聖經》有這樣的編排，背後的理念如下：

1. **從神的話語開始**：神以祂的話語創天造地，人類的幸福取決於是否聽從祂的話語。讀者先讀聖經故事，然後"背一背"金句，把神的話語藏在心裡（詩篇119:11），待人處事就有正確的標準和方向。

2. **應用神的話語**：每個單元都有一篇"品格塑造"故事或見證，跟金句主題相連，可以強化子女對這些品格的認識，學習應用神的話語。

3. **向神禱告**：禱告是人和神建立關係的不二法門，也是人向神支取力量實踐祂話語的關鍵。每個單元都有禱文一篇，供家長和子女參考，藉以親近父神。

4. **實踐神的話語**：每個單元都有三條反省問題，"想一想·做一做"為子女重溫該篇的聖經故事和品格故事或見證的內容，繼而鼓勵他們具體實踐當中的教導。

5. **以愛培育子女：**遊戲是孩童生活的一部份，家長可以藉著遊戲跟子女建立關係，也可以藉著遊戲塑造他們的品格，"童來兒嬉"正是這樣美好的親子時間。"家長提示"名副其實，是建議給家長的技巧或心法，讓家長可以從中得到啟發，明白如何塑造子女的品格。

《兒童品格聖經》裡金句的中英文版，分別取自易讀易懂的《聖經新譯本》和 *The Holy Bible, The English Standard Version 2011*。全書中英對照，能夠提高子女的語言能力。這聖經得以完成，我們不但要感謝父神在各方面的供應和帶領，也要感謝蔡文貴伉儷、劉祖湛伉儷贊助製作費，還有主編、各位編者、作者、譯者、設計同工的盡心擺上。神的兒女，無論在智慧、身體、屬靈和人際關係上都要成長，全面、全方位的成長才是神所喜悅的。願神使用這聖經建立您的子女，使他們有智慧，人見人愛，而且合神心意，正如"耶穌的智慧和身量，以及神和人對他的喜愛，都不斷增長"（路加福音2:52）。

環球聖經公會
2012年5月

x

FOREWORD
To the Parents

Through the family, God intends for us to experience the most intimate kind of human relationship. As parents, we are to raise our children up lovingly and build their character to live out God's truth and wisdom. *The CNV Kid's Bible: A Character Builder* is written with the children aged 3 to 9 in mind, as a blueprint to aid parents to fulfill their God-given duties. In this book there are 52 units, each comprising 7 sections: 1. Bible Story; 2. Verse to Know; 3. Character Builder (a moral tale or a testimony); 4. Prayer; 5. A Life Lesson (intake-output balance); 6. Hoopla Whoopee Time (games); and 7. Tips for Parents.

The CNV Kid's Bible: A Character Builder is devised with these convictions:

1. *We begin with God's Word:* Since the creation, the well being of mankind hinges upon full obedience to God's Word. To read the bible followed by verse memorization is like practicing Psalm 119:11 - hiding God's word in our hearts, having our life course set straight.

2. *We emphasize the Word's application:* Moral tales and testimonies are carefully chosen to correlate with the verses to ensure full comprehension and right application.

3. *We believe in taking prayers seriously:* Our children will learn to pray simple but constant prayers, to draw power from God in putting the moral lesson into action.

4. *We do what it takes to internalize:* "A Life Lesson" activities are designed to balance our kids' digestion and production out of the content.

5. *We hold dear the principle of learning well by having fun:* "Hoopla Whoopee Time" gives diversion to take the edge off an often-felt dryness in moral lecture. "Tips for Parents" serve to inspire more creative and dedicated efforts to guide.

The CNV Kid's Bible: A Character Builder is a full CNV/ESV 2011 bilingual reader, which has an extra bonus of heightening the children's language awareness. Indeed, we would like to thank God for His provision to see this publication through. Our gratitude especially goes to Mr and Mrs Alex Chua Boon Kwee and Mr and Mrs Lau Cho Cham for their generous endorsements. Their patience with us is profoundly appreciated. We are also grateful for the diligence of our editors, writers, translators, illustrators, designers, etc. As God's children, we know that growing in wisdom and stature, thriving in personal, relational and spiritual upping, following Jesus' suit as recorded in Luke 2:52, is at the heart of wholesome godly development. May God use our parents to help their children achieve that goal.

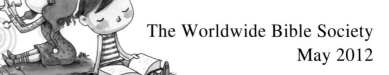

The Worldwide Bible Society
May 2012

新約篇
New Testament Stories

約瑟和馬利亞
Joseph and Mary

路加福音Luke
1:26~38, 2:1~7

馬利亞是童女，未婚夫叫約瑟。有一天，天使對馬利亞說："聖靈要臨到你，你將要懷孕生子，要給祂起名叫耶穌。"馬利亞心裡想："我還沒結婚，怎麼可能呢？"但馬利亞還是聽從天使的話，順服了神的安排。

Mary was a virgin who was to be married to Joseph. One day, an angel said to Mary, "The Holy Spirit will come upon you and you will be with child. You are to give him the name Jesus." Mary was puzzled, "How can this be, since I am not even married?" But Mary still submitted to the Lord.

後來，約瑟和馬利亞來到小鎮伯利恆，神的兒子、人類的救主耶穌基督就在馬槽裡降生了！

Later, Joseph and Mary came to the little town of Bethlehem. Jesus, the Son of God and Savior of Mankind, was born in a stable.

背一背

馬利亞說："我是主的婢女,願照你的話成就在我身上!"

路加福音1:38a

品格塑造
順服

林書豪是NBA美籍華裔球員。他曾經把打籃球放在生命中的首位,後來發現,他需要的是神。打分組賽期間,有一位牧師鼓勵他每天花一小時來親近神。他聽從了,生命也就大大更新。他說:"我學會不追逐能壞的冠冕和個人榮耀,而是學習向神擺上我的最好。"

禱告

親愛的 主耶穌,感謝你愛我,為我降生,求你給我力量學習順服你。祈禱奉耶穌的名,阿們。

And Mary said, "Behold, I am the servant of the Lord; let it be to me according to your word."

Luke 1:38a

Character Builder
To be Obedient

Jeremy Lin is one of the most famous Chinese-American NBA players. At first, he only cares about basketball. Later, he realizes that he needs God more. At the tournament games, Jeremy is urged by his pastor to spend one hour each day with God. He obeys and his life is totally renewed. He says, "I have learned not to chase after crowns that rot and rust, but give my very best to God."

Prayer

Dear Jesus, thank you for coming to this world, loving me much. Give me strength, please, to be obedient all the time. In Your name, Amen.

想一想·做一做

1. 約瑟和馬利亞順服天使的話，結果如何？

2. 林書豪聽從牧師鼓勵，帶來甚麼改變？

3. 實踐本章聖經的教導，為一位未相信耶穌的親友祈禱。

A Life Lesson

1. Both Joseph and Mary obey the angel, and what is the result?

2. Jeremy Lin listens to his pastor, what changes have come?

3. Practice: Pray for someone dear who is not a believer yet.

家長提示

要子女學會順服，家長先要讓他們知道，這樣做目的是要保護和愛他們，不是強加限制。例如：父母不准子女瀏覽某些網頁，甚至限制上網的時間，為的是不想他們接觸色情暴力的資訊，以免帶來不良的影響。家長從小事開始教導他們，子女也較容易做到。此外，多鼓勵，多幫助，能夠建立親密的關係，也有助子女順服父母。

Tips for Parents

Parents must make sure that their children learn the lesson of obedience out of love and protection, not out of oppression or manipulation. E.g., let them know the time and site allowed for net browsing are restricted because you want to protect them from bad influences. It helps when you start laying down rules as they are young. It also helps when you do it with much affirmation and loving, patient guidance.

童來兒嬉 我的禱告
Hoopla Whoopee Time *My Prayer*

請把未信耶穌的親友名字列出來，為他們禱告。

Please write down the names of family and friends who are not Christians. Pray for each.

禱告日期 *Date of Prayer*　　☆ 家人 *Family*　　　☆ 同學朋友 *Friends*

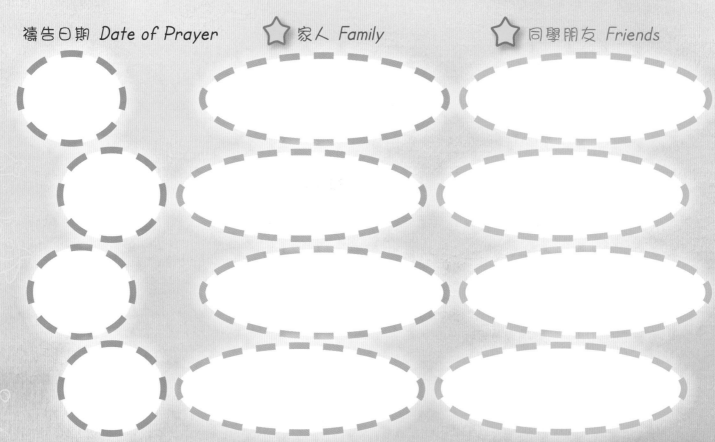

天使報佳音
The Herald of Angels

路加福音Luke
2:8~20

在伯利恆的郊外，一些牧人在晚上看守羊群。忽然，有天使站在他們旁邊，主的榮光照著他們。天使對他們說："不要怕！今天，救主基督耶穌降生了！"

忽然有一大隊天兵出現，讚美神說："在至高之處，榮耀歸與神！在地上，平安歸與他所喜悅的人！"

In the countryside of Bethlehem, some shepherds were watching over their sheep at night. Suddenly, an angel stood beside them, and the glory of God shone around them. The angels said to them, "Do not be afraid! The Savior Jesus Christ is born today!"

Suddenly there was a multitude of the heavenly host praising God and saying, "Glory to God in the highest, and on earth peace among those with whom he is pleased!"

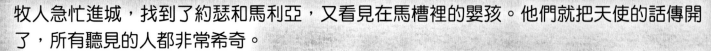

牧人急忙進城，找到了約瑟和馬利亞，又看見在馬槽裡的嬰孩。他們就把天使的話傳開了，所有聽見的人都非常希奇。

The shepherds hurried into the town and found Joseph and Mary, and saw the baby in the manger. They spread the word of the angels and all who heard the news were amazed.

忽然有一大隊天兵，同那天使一起讚美神說："在至高之處，榮耀歸與神！在地上，平安歸與他所喜悅的人！"

路加福音2:13~14

品格塑造
愛傳福音

史懷哲年青時已是出色的音樂家。神吩咐他去非洲傳福音時，他就放下一切去讀醫科，以便將來服侍非洲人。有很多人認為這是愚蠢的！但是，他認為幫助人認識神的愛比一切更重要。在幾十年的服侍裡，他不但醫好了很多患病的非洲人，也幫助他們認識神的愛，身心靈都得到健康。

禱告

親愛的主耶穌，感謝你來到世上。求你幫助我努力把這個好消息告訴別人。祈禱奉耶穌的名，阿們。

And suddenly there was with the angel a multitude of the heavenly host praising God and saying, "Glory to God in the highest, and on earth peace among those with whom he is pleased!"

Luke 2:13~14

Character Builder
To Be Gospel-sharing

Albert Schweitzer is already a brilliant musician at a young age. However, when he hears the calling of God to become a missionary in Africa, he leaves everything behind and gets retrained as a doctor to serve the Africans. Many think this is foolish, but he believes that nothing is more important than sharing the love of God. In the decades of service he makes, he not only heals the Africans who are sick, but also helps them to know the Lord and find life in Him.

Prayer

Dear Jesus, thank you for coming to this world. Help me to share your love by spreading the good news. In Your name, Amen.

想一想·做一做

1. 天使向牧羊人宣布主耶穌降生的消息，牧羊人又向別人宣告這消息。他們有甚麼共通點？

2. 史懷哲到非洲除了醫病外，還做了甚麼事？

3. 為一位未相信耶穌的親友祈禱，並且告訴那位親友有關耶穌基督的愛。

A Life Lesson

1. Upon Jesus' birth, the angels give the good news to the shepherds, and the shepherds share it with others still, what is similar in the two actions?

2. Schweitzer goes to Africa to treat patients, but what else does he do?

3. Pray for a non-believer who is a friend, go and share the love of God through Christ.

家長提示 Tips for Parents

我的女兒喜歡跟著我到處講聖經故事，做我的好幫手。我們常常一起帶著故事書和小禮物，到學校、孤兒院、醫院等地方去講故事給孩子聽。有一次，女兒問我為甚麼要這樣做，我告訴她："因為我喜歡小孩子，喜歡說故事，喜歡看見他們開心大笑。"過了一段日子，女兒跟我說："媽媽，我也有理想，將來我要開一間故事教育中心，講故事給小朋友聽，好像你一樣，要讓他們快樂。"我聽了十分感動。父母身體力行，子女受了薰陶，長大後就樂於傳福音。

My daughter keeps me company as I go about visiting orphans, bringing them gifts and telling great stories in the Bible. Once she asks me why I do such things, I tell her simply I love kids. Later, she makes up her mind that she will one day open an education center for storytelling. She wants to do what her mom has enjoyed doing – making kids happy. Parents practice what they preach, and the children will be influenced gradually to love sharing the good news.

Hoopla Whoopee Time 摺出愛心傳福音
童來兒嬉 *Fold a Paper Heart*

嘗試按以下步驟摺出你的"愛心"，寫上祝福的話，把好信息傳給別人。

Follow the steps carefully. Write a few kind words on the paper heart before you give it away

1. 先把正方形紙分成兩半，然後把兩側向後摺；
2. 把兩側向中心摺；
3. 把頂部向下摺，剛好遮蓋了三角形；
4. 把兩邊向上拉，摺出三角形；
5. 把小正方形的角向內摺，把頂部的小三角向下摺；
6. 翻到背面，就摺成一顆"愛心"了。

1. Cut a paper square into two halves, flip the corners backward.
2. Fold the corners toward the center.
3. Push open and press down the top.
4. Tuck in corners of the small squares.
5. Fold down the pointed tips.
6. Turn the paper backward to "unfold" a loving heart.

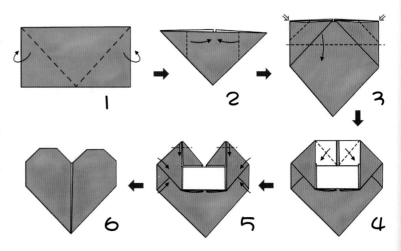

少年耶穌
Jesus the Teenager

路加福音Luke
2:41~52

耶穌十二歲時，父母帶祂上耶路撒冷過逾越節。回家途中，發現耶穌沒有和他們在一起。原來，耶穌還在聖殿裡，祂向教師提出很多問題。耶穌聰明的應對，讓所有人都感到驚訝。

When Jesus was 12 years old, his parents took him to Jerusalem for the Feast of the Passover.

On the journey home, his parents discovered that Jesus was not with them. He was actually still in the temple, asking the Rabbi many questions. Everyone was amazed at his wise responses.

馬利亞說：〝我們很擔心你！〞耶穌說：〝我必須在我父的家裡。〞耶穌順從他們，一起回家，馬利亞常記著耶穌所說的話。

Mary said to Jesus, "We are worried about you!" Jesus replied, "I had to be in my Father's house." Jesus was obedient to them and went home with them. Mary took to heart what Jesus said.

背一背

過了三天，才發現他〔耶穌〕在聖殿裡，坐在教師中間，一面聽，一面問。

路加福音2:46

品格塑造 進取

今年，我班有一位從中國北京來的新同學立君，因為他說普通話，所以常常不明白老師教授的內容，結果在第一學期考試，他除中文科外，其他的都不合格。但是他沒有灰心，反而很進取，小休時帶著書本到教員室請教老師，又常常帶著筆記本反覆溫習。學期結束時，立君由全班成績最差變為前八名，進步很快。真棒！

禱告

滿有智慧的主耶穌，你是我學習的榜樣，求你幫助我成為進取、有智慧的人。祈禱奉耶穌的名，阿們。

21

After three days they found him in the temple, sitting among the teachers, listening to them and asking them questions.

Luke 2:46

Character Builder
To Be Aspiring

Jun, a new classmate from Beijing, speaks only Mandarin and therefore fails to understand the teacher in class. It happens that his first report card tells very sad stories – all subjects failed except Chinese Language. However, he is not discouraged. On the contrary, he becomes more aspiring, taking questions to the teachers during recesses and reviewing notes anywhere he goes. As the school term nears its end, Jun is ranked the top eighth student this time. What a progress!

Prayer

O all-wise Jesus, you set the best example for me to learn. Help me become aspiring and wise. In Your name, Amen.

想一想・做一做

1. 耶穌和聖殿的教師討論信仰問題，一面專心聽，一面主動發問；立君努力學習，遇到不明白的地方就向老師請教。耶穌和立君有甚麼值得學習的地方？

2. 立君用甚麼方法使自己的學習有進步？

3. 列出三樣令你更進取，更有智慧的方法，然後在本週實踐其中一樣。

A Life Lesson

1. Jesus discusses with teachers of the law over many questions in the Temple, and Jun, too, asks when he does not understand. What can we learn from them?

2. Jun helps himself to improve by what means?

3. List three ways to make yourself become aspiring and wise. During the week, put one of these measures to practice.

家長提示 Tips for Parents

子女喜歡打破沙鍋問到底，看見新奇的事物總要問個究竟，其實這是尋求智慧的開端，是進取的表現。細心觀察，反覆思考，不斷發問，努力學習，吸取不同範疇的知識，融會貫通，實踐出來，這是得著智慧的不二法門。家長要謹記孩子每事問的時候，千萬不要說："不要再問，我怎麼知道？"如果我們真的不知道，可以跟孩子一起探索學習，尋找答案。

Children love to ask many questions; they can be quite annoying sometimes. But being inquisitive and aspiring is a necessary means of getting smart and wise. Never should a parent be deterring and utter these words: "Don't ask me again! How should I know?" In fact, we can learn with our kids when we ourselves don't have the answer!

童來兒嬉 聖經疑難逐一答
Hoopla Whoopee Time A Bible Quiz

跟子女一起尋找以下聖經問題的答案。

Look for an answer with your kids from the Bible.

1 耶穌所行的第一件神蹟是甚麼？

2 耶穌有多少個門徒？

3 以下哪個不是耶穌講的比喻？

   A. 芥菜種的比喻　　B. 浪子的比喻　　C. 約拿和大魚

4 耶穌在哪裡被釘十字架？

5 共有多少個死囚和耶穌一起釘十字架？

6 耶穌復活後和門徒相處了多少天？

1 What is Jesus' first miracle?

2 How many disciples has Jesus?

3 Which of the following is NOT a parable given by Jesus?

   A. The Mustard Seed　　B. The Prodigal Son　　C. Jonah and the Big Fish

4 Where is Jesus put on the cross?

5 How many robbers are put on the cross next to Jesus?

6 After the resurrection, how many days has Jesus lived with his disciples?

答案 Answers：
1.以水變酒 Turn water into wine　2.十二個 Twelve　3.C　4.各各他 Calvary　5.兩個 Two　6.四十天 40 days

以水變酒
Turning Water into Wine

約翰福音John
2:1~11

有人舉行婚禮，酒喝盡了。耶穌的母親請耶穌幫助，耶穌就吩咐僕人，把六口石缸倒滿清水，他們就這樣作了。耶穌又吩咐僕人，把缸裡的水舀給總管喝，僕人又這樣作了。

At the wedding, the wine was all gone. Jesus told the servants to fill six stone jars full with water. They did so and then Jesus told them to draw some water out to give to the master of banquet. The servants did as they were told.

總管嘗了一口，說："這真是上好的美酒啊！" 將水變成酒，這是耶穌在加利利所行的第一件神蹟。

The master of banquet took a taste and said, "This is the best wine!" Turning water into wine was the first miracle that Jesus performed.

背一背

施比受更為有福。

使徒行傳20:35b

品格塑造
樂於助人

妹妹今年剛升小學一年級，媽媽買了新文具給她，讓她開開心心上學去。三星期後，媽媽責備妹妹不好好愛惜文具，把橡皮擦分成四小塊，還有一小塊不見掉。妹妹大哭起來，說："坐在我旁邊的女同學很窮，沒錢買橡皮擦，所以把作業擦得很髒，我就把自己的橡皮擦分成四小塊，送一塊給她回家用，一塊上學時用，現在她的作業都很整潔了！"

媽媽聽後，知道妹妹這樣幫人，就向妹妹道歉，並送那個同學一套全新的文具套裝。

Walk with Jesus

禱告

親愛的主耶穌，感謝你常常幫助我。求你教我能像你一樣樂於助人，實踐神的愛。祈禱奉耶穌的名，阿們。

29

Verse to Know

It is more blessed to give than to receive.

Acts 20:35b

Character Builder
To Be Helpful

Cissy is a first grader, and her mom buys her a new stationery set to make her happy. Three weeks later, mom gets cross and is harsh on Cissy because she cuts the eraser into four pieces and, worse still, one is gone. Cissy is in tears as she explains: "The girl who sits next to me is very poor, she has not an eraser to help keep her work tidy. I cut my own into pieces to share with her, and now her homework is all nice and clean."

Since Cissy is helpful, mom tells Cissy she is sorry, and she buys that poor classmate another stationery set as a gift.

Prayer

Dear Jesus, You are a wonderful helper. Help me to become like you, always helpful and loving. In Your name, Amen.

想一想．做一做

1. 耶穌怎樣幫助人解決沒酒的問題？

2. 妹妹為甚麼要把橡皮擦分成四小塊？媽媽為甚麼責備她？

3. 在本週內最少幫助一個人，然後記下幫助人的經過和感受。

A Life Lesson

1. How does Jesus solve the problem when the wine is gone?

2. Why does Cissy cut her eraser into four pieces? Why is mom angry at her?

3. Help someone over the week. Write down what happens and how you feel.

Walk with Jesus

家長提示　Tips for Parents

你的子女是否樂於助人？如果你希望子女成為快樂的人，就要多鼓勵他們幫助別人，因為"助人為快樂之本"，幫助別人有助子女建立自信心和同理心，這比起物質獎賞的功效來得更持久，更使人快樂。在經濟掛帥的社會裡，我們更需要教導子女無條件地幫助人，不計回報，不然子女就難以成為真正快樂的人。送你三個樂於助人小錦囊：1.幫助人不要等，立即行動；2.量力而為；3.助人不張揚，不指望回報。

Is your child always helpful? If you want your kid to be happy, you must encourage her to be available to others. When helping others, we get more confident and become empathetic. This brings lasting rewards more so than do material goods. Train up your child: 1. Help others now, don't wait; 2. Help, but know your limits; 3. Help, but make no fuss about it; still, don't look for any returns.

童來兒嬉 互相幫助
Hoopla Whoopee Time *Help One Another*

二人或三人一組，輪流說希望幫對方一個忙，對方一定要答應，助人者必須立即行動。看看以下兩個例子：

In groups of 2 or 3, take turns to offer to help, the other party must oblige, and the helpful deed must be carried out right away. See these examples:

甲：你渴了，我幫你倒一杯水好嗎？
乙：好吧，謝謝你！
甲：不用客氣。

A : Are you thirsty? Let me pour a glass of water for you.
B : Good. Thanks.
A : You are welcome.

乙：你累了，我替你按摩肩膊好嗎？
丙：好啊，謝謝你！
乙：我很樂意幫助你！

A : You look tired. Shall I massage your shoulders?
B : Thanks… Oooh…
A : I'm just glad to help.

遊戲目的：藉著互相服侍，一起實踐樂於助人的精神。
Purpose: To serve one another, to make oneself available.

治好大臣的兒子
Healing the Official's Son

約翰福音John
4:46~54

有 一個大臣，他的兒子在迦百農患了重病，快要死了。他來見耶穌，求耶穌醫治他的兒子。

耶穌對他說："你回去吧，你的兒子好了。"大臣相信耶穌的話，就回去了。還在路上，他的僕人就走過來，說："孩子好了！"

There was a royal official whose son in Capernaum was seriously ill and close to death. He came to Jesus and begged him to heal his son.

Jesus said to him, "You may go. Your son is healed." The official believed in Jesus' words and returned home. On the way, he met his servants, who told him, "Your son is well!"

那孩子好轉過來，正是耶穌說話的時間。於是，大臣和他全家都相信了耶穌。這是耶穌回到加利利以後所行的第二件神蹟。

The boy had become better just at the time when Jesus was speaking. So the official and his whole household came to faith in Jesus. This is the second miracle that Jesus performed after he returned to Galilee.

背一背

| 這父親就知道，那正是耶穌告訴他"你的兒子好了"的時候，他自己和全家就信了。

約翰福音4:53

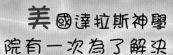

品格塑造
信靠

Abba Father

美國達拉斯神學院有一次為了解決經濟危機而召開祈禱會，其中一位講師祈禱說："神啊！千山上的牛羊都是你的，求你賣掉一些來幫助我們。"大約同時，一位農場主人剛賣了兩車牲口，他認為神感動他要把款項奉獻，就專程到神學院去。接待員收到支票後隨即交給院長，院長看看金額正是他們需要的款項，再看看簽名，認出是他的朋友，就對那位講師說："神剛賣掉祂的牛羊來幫助我們。"

信靠的對象是神，祂是十分豐足的。

禱告

親愛的天父，感謝你是豐足的，求你教導我認識你，因而增加對你的信靠。祈禱奉耶穌的名，阿們。

The father knew that was the hour when Jesus had said to him, "Your son will live." And he himself believed, and all his household.

John 4:53

Character Builder
To Be Trusting

A financial crisis emerges at Dallas Theological Seminary, therefore a prayer meeting is called for. A professor prays, "O God, the cattle on a thousand hills is yours, have some sold to help us!" At about the same time, a farm owner has had two truckloads of cattle sold. And he feels called by God to donate some money, so he goes straight to the seminary. The receptionist takes his check to the president, who recognizes this being his friend's, and he hails, "God just sold some in the herds to help us indeed!"

God is the one in whom we have full faith; He is an abundant God!

Prayer

Dear Father God, you are bountiful. Teach me to know you through your Word, and gain faith. In Jesus' name, Amen.

想一想．做一做

1. 從哪裡可以看出大臣對主耶穌有信心？

2. 故事裡的院長對神有信心嗎？從哪裡可以得知？

3. 增加對神的信心就要增加對神的認識，本週背誦三節金句。

A Life Lesson

1. How can you tell the official has strong faith in Jesus?

2. The President in the character story has faith in God. Do you agree? How do you know?

3. To know God and gain faith, you must know His Word. Memorize three verses during the week.

Abba Father

家長提示

人懂得信靠神，不是因為自己有甚麼才幹或資源，而是願意謙卑面對自己的不足，等候神的引領。家長要教導子女認識神，這是舉足輕重的。跟子女共同面對成功和失敗，並藉此操練對神的信心，比起只尋求成功更重要。

Tips for Parents

Trust accomplishes more than do being talented and resourceful. A person with full faith can face his own inadequacy. With humility he gets guidance from God to achieve what needs being done. Parents should learn this lesson with their children. Face inadequacies and failures with faith in God, this will lead to a path that gains more than success.

童來兒嬉 找不同
Hoopla Whoopee Time *Find the Differences*

 請從兩幅圖中，找出四個不同之處。

Please find four differences from the two pictures.

得人漁夫
A Fisher of Men

路加福音Luke
5:1~11

耶穌坐在西門的船上教導眾人。講完了,耶穌對彼得說:"把船開到水深的地方。"彼得說:"我昨晚一條魚都打不上來,不過,我願意聽從你說的話下網。"

彼得一下子就網住了很多的魚,甚至連漁網都幾乎裂開了!船也重得往下沉,所有的人都十分驚訝。

Jesus sat in the boat of Simon Peter and taught the people. After he finished speaking, he told Peter, "Move the boat to deeper water." Peter said, "I had caught nothing last night, but I will let down the nets because you say so."

Peter put down the nets and immediately caught so many fish that the nets began to break. Even the boats began to sink under the load. Everyone was amazed.

彼得立即俯伏在耶穌的腳前，說："主啊，離開我，我是罪人！"耶穌說："不要怕！從今以後，你要作得人的漁夫了。"

Peter immediately fell at Jesus' feet and said, "Lord, go away from me, for I am a sinner!" Jesus said, "Do not be afraid. From now on, you will be a fisher of men."

背一背

你們應當順服神。

雅各書4:7a

品格塑造
順服

鳥媽媽生了一群小鳥。有一天，鳥媽媽教牠們學飛，要牠們從高處跳下，然後不停拍動翅膀，直至能飛到高空為止。小鳥當中，阿高最不願意這樣練習，牠跟媽媽說："這樣練習，還未能飛就摔死啦！"媽媽說："這高度不會摔壞你。如果你不會飛，狐狸隨時都能跑來吃掉你！"可是阿高寧願留在巢內不學飛。

有一天，狐狸趁鳥媽媽外出找食物的時候，真的爬到樹上來捉小鳥！其他小鳥一下子就飛走了，但是阿高不敢飛出鳥巢，最後就被狐狸捉去了！

禱告

親愛的天父，感謝你讓我聽到彼得的故事，求你教導我順服你，像彼得聽從耶穌一樣。祈禱奉耶穌的名，阿們。

Verse to Know

Submit yourselves therefore to God.

James 4:7a

Character Builder
To Be Obedient

Mother Bird has many chicks. One day she decides to teach them to fly. She makes them jump off from a high place, flap their wings until they go up in the air. Among these chicks, Algo is the one most unwilling to try. "We'll die from falling," he protests. But Mother Bird reassures, "At this height you won't. But if you don't try to learn, you'll have no chance of taking flight from danger." Still, Algo would not listen to his mom.

One day, Mr Fox sneaks behind the nest while Mother Bird is away looking for food. All the little birds fly away to escape easily, but Algo is taken by the predator.

Prayer

Dear Father God, thanks for this fisher story. Have me obey your commands the way Peter obeyed your Son Jesus. In Jesus' name, Amen.

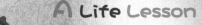

1. 假如你是彼得，你願意順服耶穌的吩咐嗎？為甚麼？
2. 小鳥阿高為甚麼不聽媽媽的話？結果如何？
3. 寫出三樣順服父母的困難，然後想想怎樣改善。

A Life Lesson

1. If you were Peter, would you obey Jesus? Why?
2. Why does Algo not listen to his mom? What happens in the end?
3. What three lessons of disobedience have you learned? How have you been making progress?

家長提示 Tips for Parents

"自我中心"是順服的強敵，不論成人或小孩子都容易犯上"自以為是"的毛病。這毛病引致的後果可大可小，所以不要過分保護子女，要讓他們從錯誤中學習謙卑，明白神才是智慧的根源，使他們漸漸學懂順服的功課。

For adults or kids, the greatest enemy of obedience is self-centeredness, which can cause harmful consequences. Do not overprotect your children; do let them learn from mistakes, learn to obey by embracing humility and relying on God, the fountain of wisdom.

童來兒嬉 順服立志卡
Hoopla Whoopee Time *An I-Pledge-to-Obey Card*

在魚身上寫下立志的話，求天父幫助你順服，不堅持自以為是。

Write down your pledge to obey on the fish below. Ask God to help you unlearn the self-centered habits.

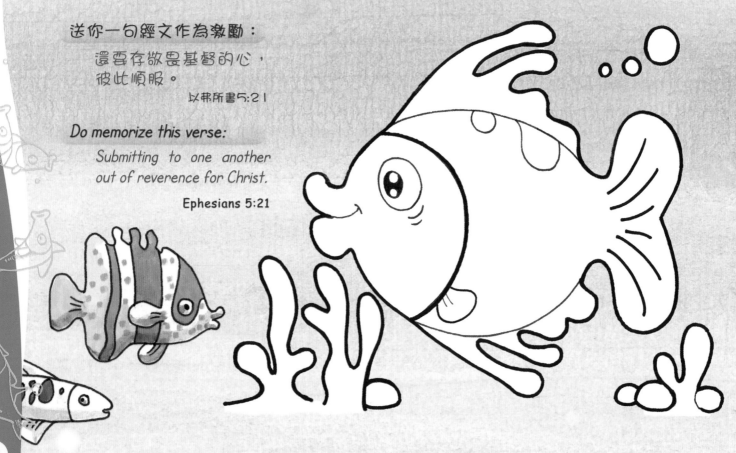

送你一句經文作為激勵：

> 還要存敬畏基督的心，
> 彼此順服。
>
> 以弗所書5:21

Do memorize this verse:

> Submitting to one another
> out of reverence for Christ.
>
> Ephesians 5:21

癱子和四個朋友
The Paralytic and Four Men

馬可福音Mark
2:1~12

耶穌回到迦百農，大家來聽祂講道，由於人太多，連門前的地方都沒有了。有四個人同心合力把一個癱子抬來，又把房頂拆通了，將癱子連人帶褥子縋下去。耶穌看見他們的信心，說："孩子，你的罪赦了！"

Jesus returned to Capernaum. The people gathered together to listen to his teaching. There were so many people that there was no room, not even outside the door. Four men came, carrying a paralytic. They made a hole in the roof and lowered the paralytic on a mat into the house. Jesus saw their faith and said, "Son, your sins are forgiven."

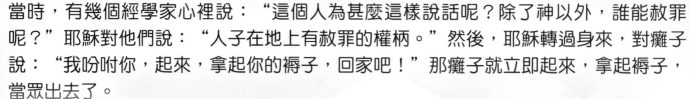

當時，有幾個經學家心裡說：「這個人為甚麼這樣說話呢？除了神以外，誰能赦罪呢？」耶穌對他們說：「人子在地上有赦罪的權柄。」然後，耶穌轉過身來，對癱子說：「我吩咐你，起來，拿起你的褥子，回家吧！」那癱子就立即起來，拿起褥子，當眾出去了。

Some of the teachers of the law thought to themselves, "Why does Jesus talk like that? Who can forgive sins but God alone?" Jesus said to them, "The Son of Man has authority on earth to forgive sins." He then turned and said to the paralytic, "I tell you, get up, take your mat and go home!" The paralytic stood up immediately, picked up his mat and walked out in front of everyone.

53

眾人都非常驚奇，稱頌神，說："我們從來沒有見過這樣的事。"
The people were amazed and praised God, saying "We have never seen anything like this!"

勸你們大家要同心，在你們中間不要分黨，只要在同一的心思、同一的意念上團結起來。

哥林多前書1:10b

品格塑造
合群

英國的冬天會突然出現大風雪，天氣突然變冷，很多牛就會死去。但有一種牛，是"赫里福"品種的，每當牠們遇見大風雪時就會肩並肩，藉著互相取暖來保持體溫，因而不會大量死亡。

當我們面對困難時，團結合群就是力量。

禱告

慈愛的天父，感謝你賜我朋友和家人，求主賜我們團結合群的心，幫助更多人。祈禱奉耶穌的名，阿們。

And that there be no divisions among you, but that you be united in the same mind and the same judgment.

1 Corinthians 1:10b

Character Builder
To Be Sociable

During winter in England, there are sudden snow storms. The cold weather causes the death of many cattle. But the Hereford breed of cattle knows how to stay alive. They will stand shoulder to shoulder in a snow storm to keep warm.

When facing difficulties, we need to be sociable and pull our strength together.

Prayer

O loving God, thank you for giving me a family and friends. Make us always united in spirit to do good to others. In Jesus' name, Amen.

想一想・做一做

1. 癱子的朋友怎樣發揮團結合群精神幫助他？

2. "赫里福" 品種的牛怎樣抵禦寒冷？

3. 你可以跟朋友一起做甚麼事，來幫助身邊的人？

A Life Lesson

1. How do the friends of the paralyzed man show that they are united in faith and action?

2. How does the Hereford breed brave the severe cold weather?

3. What can you and your friends do together to help those who are in need?

家長提示 Tips for Parents

記得小時候，鄰舍總是團結合群、彼此相助的。我媽媽經常會幫鄰舍暫時照顧小孩，大家的小孩一起玩耍，關係要好。隨著社會變遷，現在的鄰舍各不相熟，更遑論團結相助。要子女學習團結合群，可以讓他們經歷合作帶來的快樂，從中學習放下自己，擴闊世界觀，逐漸盛載更多的人和事。

When I was little, my neighbors were sociable and banded together all the time. My mom would take care of someone else's kids; the elder ones would look after their younger siblings. But because time has changed, what we call neighbors nowadays are practical strangers. Teach your children about unity by having them work with others for others. Let them struggle to put themselves down, embrace a bigger world with a common good where the joy of acceptance and tolerance is a daily experience.

童來兒嬉 Hoopla Whoopee Time 團結合群拼出守望圖 Building a Puzzle

複印以下拼圖兩份，剪成紙塊，再隨意把部件分給兩人或兩組。須團結合作，交出對方需要的部件，合力完成。

Make copies of the following picture. Cut them into pieces, then randomly share with a teammate. Exchange one with another for pieces needed to complete the puzzle.

寡婦的兒子復活
The Resurrection of the Widow's Son

路加福音Luke
7:11~17

耶穌往拿因城去，快到城門的時候，有些人把一個死人抬了出來，他是獨生子，他的母親是寡婦，大家都很傷心地哭泣。

Jesus went to a town called Nain. As he came near the town gate, a dead man was being carried out. He was the only son of a widow. Everyone was crying sadly.

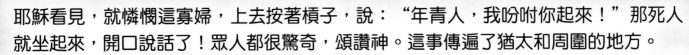

耶穌看見，就憐憫這寡婦，上去按著槓子，說："年青人，我吩咐你起來！" 那死人就坐起來，開口說話了！眾人都很驚奇，頌讚神。這事傳遍了猶太和周圍的地方。

Jesus saw this and he had compassion on the widow. He put his hand on the coffin and said, "Young man, I say to you, get up!" The dead man sat up and began to talk! Everyone was amazed and praised God. The news about this event spread throughout Judea and the surrounding areas.

背一背

主看見了，就憐憫她，對她說："不要哭！"

路加福音7:13

品格塑造

憐憫

工業革命時，英國人雷克斯看到很多童工，每天在工廠辛苦工作，星期天休息時則四處遊蕩。於是，他聘請了幾位婦女，在家中讓孩童上課，又教他們學習聖經。雷克斯因為憐憫孩童，不想他們學壞就創辦了主日學，從此各地的教會也漸漸辦起主日學來了。

禱告

親愛的天父，感謝你藉著雷克斯的手創辦了主日學，求你教我怎樣將憐憫變成行動，幫助有需要的人。祈禱奉耶穌的名，阿們。

And when the Lord saw her, he had compassion on her and said to her, "Do not weep."

Luke 7:13

Character Builder
To Be Compassionate

During the Industrial Revolution, Robert Raikes, an Englishman, saw many child laborers wander in the streets with nothing to do on Sundays. Using his own money, Raikes employed a few women to teach the children Bible at homes. Raikes had compassion on these children, not wanting them to turn rotten. Gradually Sunday Schools became the work of the churches in different parts of the world.

Prayer

Dear Father God, thank you for Raikes, who helped found the Sunday Schools. Put compassion in my heart to help the needy. In Jesus' name, Amen.

想一想·做一做

1. 耶穌為甚麼幫助那個寡婦？

2. 雷克斯如何將憐憫變成行動，幫助孩童？

3. 留意本週的新聞，有哪宗令你動了慈心？在"童來兒嬉"貼上那則新聞剪報，並寫下感受。

A Life Lesson

1. Why does Jesus help the widow?

2. How did Raikes put compassion on children into action?

3. In the newspaper, find a story that stirs a compassion. Make a clip, and write down your feelings.

家長提示 Tips for Parents

教導子女憐憫別人，可先培養他們的同理心。家長可以跟他們講述一些感人的故事，然後引導他們站在當事人的立場去想像，他們會有甚麼感受。經過長期引導，他們懂得將心比己，就會作出適切的愛心行動。

A lesson on compassion starts with empathy toward others. Do tell touching stories of any kind to your kids; put them in the shoes of the story characters and let them search their feelings. Over a period, they should be more able to take compassion on people.

童來兒嬉 關心身邊事
Hoopla Whoopee Time Learn About the News

留意本週新聞，有哪宗令你動了慈心？在下面貼上剪報，寫下感受，並想像如果有機會，你會怎樣幫助故事中人。

Make a newspaper clip out of a story of compassion. Write down your feelings, imagine what you would do to help.

如果有機會，我會這樣幫助：
Given a chance to help, I would ...

五餅二魚
Five Loaves and Two Fish

馬太福音Matthew
14:13~21

耶穌在曠野講論神的國，人數超過五千。快到晚上了，耶穌吩咐門徒給眾人東西吃。門徒說："不行啊，這裡是曠野，天已經很晚了。"有個小男孩帶來五個餅和兩條魚。耶穌拿起餅和魚，望著天，祝福了，就由門徒分給眾人吃。

Jesus spoke to people about the Kingdom of God in a remote place. There were more than five thousand men. As the evening approached, Jesus told his disciples to give the people something to eat. The disciples said, "We cannot do that, this is an isolated place and the day is now over." A little boy was there, who had five loaves and two fish. Jesus took the loaves and fish. Looking up to heaven, he gave thanks and then gave the loaves and fish to the disciples to distribute to the people.

大家都吃飽了！還剩下很多零碎的，裝滿了十二個籃子。

The people all ate to their full and left over many pieces, enough to fill twelve baskets.

你們要把一切憂慮卸給神，因為他顧念你們。

彼得前書5:7

品格塑造
體貼

志明的果園收成豐富。他知道鄰居的老婆婆病了，就送她一些柑子。老婆婆看著柑子，想起失去小狗的女孩，於是拿了兩個柑子給小女孩。

小女孩覺得獨居的伯伯比她更有需要，於是把柑子送給伯伯。伯伯看著柑子，想起昨天扶他一把的年輕人，就把柑子拿給他。

這個年輕人竟然是志明！志明把柑子放在一旁，看著看著，覺得很甘甜，因為這是顧念體貼人的果子呀！

禱告

親愛的天父，感謝你讓我認識五餅二魚的神蹟，求你教導我顧念體貼別人的需要，讓別人感受到你的愛。祈禱奉耶穌的聖名，阿們。

Casting all your anxieties on him, because he cares for you.

1 Peter 5:7

Character Builder
To Be Considerate

Ming has a full harvest in his garden. He knows that his neighbor the old lady is ill, so he gives her some tangerines. The old lady looks at the tangerines and remembers the little girl who has lost her dog, so she gives two tangerines to the little girl.

The little girl thinks that the old gentleman living on his own is more needy than herself, so she gives her tangerines to him. The old gentleman looks at the tangerines and thinks of the young man who lends a helping hand the other day, so he gives the tangerines to him.

That young man is Ming! Ming puts the tangerines aside and looks at them. He finds that very sweet, because the fruit of being nice and considerate is being harvested.

Prayer

Dear Father God, thank you for showing me the miracle of the five loaves and two fish. Teach me to be sensitive to other people's need so that they can feel your love. In Jesus' name, Amen.

想－想·做－做

1. 如果你是五餅二魚神蹟中的小男孩，你願意和別人分享餅和魚嗎？為甚麼？

2. 品格故事中為甚麼沒有人吃柑子？

3. 畫一張心意卡，送給你所愛的家人或朋友，表示關心、體貼他的需要。

A Life Lesson

1. If you were the boy in the story of the five loaves and two fish, would you be willing to share with others? Why?

2. In the character builder story, why does no one eat the tangerines?

3. Draw a card and give it to your family or a friend to show your care.

家長提示 Tips for Parents

子女獨自擁有很多東西，要教導他們體貼別人的需要，懂得分享的確不容易。其實，在買玩具時，不妨選擇一些要和別人一起玩耍的玩具，例如：飛行棋。藉著這類遊戲，子女可以學習分享，並感受箇中樂趣，在遊樂中培養品格，一舉兩得。

Children nowadays own so many things, so it is difficult to teach them about considering others' needs and being willing to share. Here is a small tip: when buying toys, choose toys which require kids to play with others, such as board games. Using these games, the children learn to share and enjoy the experience. They can build up their character during play time.

童來兒嬉 我的繽紛小魚
Hoopla Whoopee Time *My Colorful Fish*

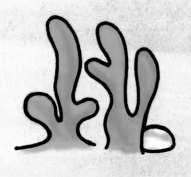

家長引導子女玩這個遊戲：

1 講出曾經或願意和人分享的一件東西。

2 講完了，就把一片魚鱗填上顏色。

看看能不能把兩尾小魚都填上繽紛的色彩。

The adults lead the children to play this game:

1 Mention a thing that you have shared or would like to share with someone.

2 Then color a fish scale.

See if you can make two colorful fish.

魚嘴巴裡的銀幣
The Coin in the Mouth of the Fish

馬太福音Matthew
17:24~27

收稅的人來問彼得："你們的老師不交稅嗎？"彼得說："交"。

耶穌問彼得："地上的君王收稅，是向自己的兒子，還是外人呢？"彼得回答說："是外人。"耶穌就說："這樣，兒子就可以免稅了。"

A tax collector came and asked Peter, "Doesn't your teacher pay the tax?" Peter replied, "Yes, he does."

Jesus asked Peter, "From whom do the kings of the earth collect taxes? From their own sons or from others?" Peter replied, "From others." Jesus said, "Then the sons are exempt."

但是為免觸怒他們，耶穌又說：“不過，你還是去海邊釣魚吧，把第一條魚的嘴巴打開，你就會發現裡面有一個大銀幣，足夠你和我的稅款了。”

However, not to give offense to them, Jesus also said to Peter, "But go to the sea and fish. Open the mouth of the first fish that you catch and you will find a coin there, enough for my tax and yours."

背一背

你們為主的緣故，要順服人的一切制度。

彼得前書2:13a

品格塑造
順服

一天晚上，寄宿生志文睡不著，就跑到學校的跳水館，他想半夜跳水，不會有人看見的。他爬上十米高的跳臺，正準備跳下去時，才看見身邊有張告示寫著"禁止跳水"。原來水池正在維修，裡面沒有水，那時他抹了一把汗。

規則不是要為難我們，順服規則是為了保護我們和防止混亂。

禱告

親愛的主耶穌，感謝你以身作則，求你幫助我學習順服你，作美好的見證。祈禱奉耶穌的名，阿們。

Verse to Know

Be subject for the Lord's sake to every human institution.

1 Peter 2:13a

Character Builder
To Be Obedient

One night, John, a school boarder, can't sleep so he goes to the diving pool, climbs up the 10 meter diving board, and prepares to dive, disregarding the "No Diving" sign. But then there is a voice in his mind telling him to obey rules. So he climbs back down instead. As he walks past the pool, he has a chill. The pool is being repaired and there is no water in it!

We have rules in our homes and schools. These are not to make it difficult for us, but to protect us and to prevent disorder.

Prayer

Dear Jesus, thank you for being a model. Help me to obey you, and bear good testimony. In Your name, Amen.

想一想・做一做

1. 耶穌既然是神的兒子，理應不用交稅，為甚麼祂還是繳交了？

2. 如果你是志文，你會不會守規則？為甚麼？

3. 你曾經因為不守規則而受罰嗎？試說出事情的經過。

A Life Lesson

1. You would think Jesus, the Son of God, could not care less about paying taxes, but why did Jesus still bother?

2. If you were John, would you break the rules anyway? Why?

3. Were you ever punished for breaking rules? What happened?

家長提示 Tips for Parents

老人家常說"小時偷針，大時偷金"，意思是要從年幼時就學會順服，守規則不要因為子女年輕犯小錯就以為不要緊。無論是在家裡，或是在主日學，都要跟小孩子訂立規則，大家都認真遵守。家長和導師要以身作則，賞罰分明，才能使小孩子明白守法的重要。

An old Chinese saying goes: A boy who steals a needle might steal gold when he gets old. This of course is to capitalize on obeying rules. Do let your children know they must do their best to abide by the rules. Set examples and reward properly, so that children can fully appreciate the significance.

童來兒嬉 約法三章
Hoopla Whoopee Time *Make a Pact*

跟子女一起訂立規則，以三至五條為限，並且一起努力實踐遵行。

Make a pact with your children. Set a few rules together and carry them out sincerely.

我們的法則 *Our Rules*

1. . . . .

2. . . . .

3. . . . .

4. . . . .

5. . . . .

宗旨：共同遵守・一視同仁
Objective: All Is Keeping, Treat all alike

平息風浪
Calming the Storm

馬可福音Mark
6:45~52

耶穌叫門徒上船到伯賽大去，自己卻往山上禱告。整個晚上，因為風向不順，海浪很大，門徒搖櫓搖得很辛苦。這一切，耶穌都看見了。

天快亮的時候，耶穌在海面行走，往門徒那裡去。門徒以為見了鬼怪，就很害怕，耶穌安慰他們不用害怕。

Jesus told the disciples to get into the boat and go on to Bethsaida, while he went up onto the mountain to pray. During the whole evening the wind was against them and the waves were high. Jesus saw the disciples straining at the oars.

Near the time of dawn, Jesus went out to the disciples, walking on the water. The disciples saw him and were afraid, thinking that he was a ghost. Jesus comforted them not to be afraid.

耶穌上了船，和門徒在一起，風浪立即就平靜了。門徒十分驚訝，因為他們的心還是遲鈍。

Jesus got on the boat with the disciples and immediately the wind and the waves died down. The disciples were amazed because their hearts were still hardened.

耶穌立刻對他們說："放心吧！是我，不要怕。"

馬可福音6:50b

品格塑造
信靠

小猴愛在森林裡從樹頂跳下來，讓猴媽媽抱在懷裡。媽媽抱著小猴，小猴總會哈哈大笑。

有一天，猴叔叔來探望小猴，看見小猴在玩這遊戲，就想跟小猴玩一趟。怎料小猴嚷著："不要叔叔，只要媽媽！"不管叔叔怎樣哄牠逗牠，小猴都不願意。叔叔問："為甚麼呢？"媽媽笑著回答："因為小猴熟悉自己的媽媽，也信靠媽媽呢。"

禱告

親愛的天父，感謝你，因為你是我信心的源頭，求你幫助我面對各種困難。祈禱奉耶穌的名，阿們。

But immediately he (Jesus) spoke to them and said, "Take heart; it is I. Do not be afraid."

Mark 6:50b

Character Builder
To Be Trusting

Monkey Little loves to swing on trees, letting himself fall on Mommy's lap. Lying in her arms, he would grin his approval and delight.

One day, Uncle comes for a visit to play with Little. Out of the blue the chimp yearns for its mother. No matter what Uncle does, Little is not pleased. Uncle exclaims, "What happens?" Mother says smilingly, "Little knows not anybody else to trust; he has faith in Mommy alone."

Prayer

Dear Father God, thank you for being my source of faith. Make me strong in the face of any challenges. In Jesus' name, Amen.

想一想・做一做

1. 門徒為甚麼對耶穌沒有信心?

2. 小猴為甚麼不願意跟猴叔叔玩遊戲?

3. 你或親友有沒有遇上甚麼困難?將這事告訴天父,求祂賜信心和智慧去解決。

A Life Lesson

1. Why do the disciples have little faith in Jesus?

2. Why does Monkey Little not play with Uncle the tricks he loves so much?

3. Do you or your friends have any difficulties to overcome? Tell that to Father God in prayer, asking for faith and wisdom.

家長提示

對人和神的信靠是累積得來的。由小問題開始,家長和子女一起想辦法;然後慢慢放手,漸漸多讓子女自己動腦筋,想出解決的方法,家長則從旁提點。久而久之,可以增強子女的自信心。要培養子女對神對人的信心,辦法也差不多,多些讓他們經歷神和人的幫助,經歷多了,他們對神和人就越來越有信心。

Tips for Parents

Trust increases little by little. When there is a small challenge, parents should work it out together with their children; and later letting go, they help by guiding them to work on their own, with prayers unto God, of course. Over the time, the children will learn to trust in themselves, in their parents, and in God most of all.

童來兒嬉 Hoopla Whoopee Time 心中的風浪 A Storm Within

在圖中的波浪裡，寫下你最近遇到的困難，然後告訴爸媽，並一起祈禱。

Outline your problems in the space of surging waves below. Share with your parents; pray together for strong faith.

浪子回頭
The Prodigal Son

路加福音Luke
15:11~24

有 一位父親，他有兩個兒子，小兒子要求分家業，父親就把財產分給他。小兒子收拾行李，到遠方去了。

A father had two sons. The younger son wanted his share of the estate. So the father gave his share to him. The younger son packed and set off to a distant place.

在那裡，他把錢財花光了。小兒子很窮困，去幫人家放豬，恨不得吃豬所吃的豆莢，但沒有人給他吃。

There he wasted his money. The young son became poor. He worked as a hired hand, feeding pigs. He longed to eat the pods that the pigs were eating, but no one gave him any.

小兒子想念父親，也知道自己錯了，於是就回家去。父親遠遠看見，就跑過去，抱住他，不停地和他親吻。父親不但原諒了他，還為他設宴慶祝。

He thought of his father and knew that he had done wrong. So he returned home. His father saw him from far away and ran to him. The father embraced the son and kissed him. The father not only forgave him, but also held a feast to celebrate.

我們若承認自己的罪，神是信實的、公義的，必定赦免我們的罪，潔淨我們脫離一切不義。

約翰壹書1:9

品格塑造
知錯能改

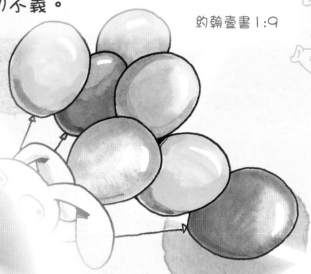

美國第一任總統華盛頓小時候十分頑皮，一次趁爸爸不在家，用斧子把爸爸心愛的小櫻桃樹砍斷了。爸爸回家發現樹倒了，大大發怒。華盛頓知道自己做錯了，就勇敢地承認過失，準備接受責罰。爸爸給他真誠知錯能改的心感動了，原諒了他。另外一次在春天，表哥給他一個大蘋果，華盛頓不願意和大家分享，除非爸爸把果園裡的蘋果都送他。後來華盛頓回想這事，不禁羞愧起來，於是向爸爸認錯，答應以後不再自私。

禱告

親愛的天父，感謝你，因為你樂意赦免人的罪。求你原諒我犯的過錯，教導我勇於認錯，並且改過。祈禱奉耶穌的名，阿們。

If we confess our sins, he is faithful and just to forgive us our sins and to cleanse us from all unrighteousness.

1 John 1:9

Character Builder
To Be Repentant

Washington, the first American president, was very naughty as a young boy. Once when his father was not at home, he chopped down his father's beloved cherry tree with an axe. His father was very angry when he got home and found the fallen tree. Washington knew that he had done wrong and bravely admitted his fault. He was ready to accept his punishment. His father was moved by his true repentance and forgave him. At another time in spring, his cousin gave him a big apple and he was not willing to share it with the others, unless his father gave him all the apples in the orchard. Later, when Washington thought about this, he was very ashamed and apologized to his father, promising that he would never be selfish again.

Prayer

Dear *Father God,* thank you for forgiving sins. Teach me to confess my wrongdoing bravely and correct my mistakes. In Jesus' name, Amen.

想一想・做一做

1. 小兒子回家認錯，得到甚麼對待？

2. 如果你是華盛頓的爸爸，你會原諒兒子的過失嗎？為甚麼？

3. 你最近有沒有做錯事？你已認錯嗎？試把認錯的話寫下來，向天父認錯。

A Life Lesson

1. The younger son returns home to admit his wrong. How is he treated then?

2. If you were Washington's father, would you forgive your son's mistakes? Why?

3. Have you done anything wrong recently? Have you admitted your fault? Try to write down your apology and pray to Father in Heaven for forgiveness.

家長提示

專家指出，孩子從三歲起就曉得說謊，要教導他們知錯能改，真不容易。給你們一個提示，時常提醒子女"天父住在心裡"，如果他們撒謊，就使天父傷心。要常常跟子女一起祈禱，培養他們願意向天父坦誠認錯的品格。

Tips for Parents

Experts tell us children know how to lie from the age of three. It is not easy to teach them to truly admit their wrongs. Here is a tip: often remind your children that Heavenly Father lives in their hearts. If they lie, the Father will be sad. Often pray with the children so that they learn to freely admit their wrongs to the Father in Heaven, without holding back.

童來兒嬉 浪子迷宮
Hoopla Whoopee Time *Return of the Prodigal Son*

小兒子知錯了，請幫助他回家向爸爸認錯吧！

The young son knows he has done wrong. Help him to get home to apologize to his father.

財主和拉撒路
The Rich Man and Lazarus

路加福音Luke
16:19~31

有 一個財主，穿著華麗的衣服，天天宴樂。又有個乞丐，名叫拉撒路，滿身生瘡，天天在財主的門口討飯，有狗來舔他的瘡，財主卻沒憐憫他。

A rich man was dressed in fine clothes and lived in luxury every day. There was also a beggar called Lazarus, who was covered with sores. Every day he sat outside the rich man's gate to beg for food. Even the dogs came to lick his sores, and the rich man did not show mercy to him.

後來，乞丐死了，在亞伯拉罕的懷裡享受安息；財主也死了，卻去了陰間受苦，那裡的火焰很大。財主叫苦連天。

The beggar died and was carried to Abraham's side and was comforted. The rich man also died, but was tormented in hell, where the flame was great. The rich man was in great pain.

憐憫人的人有福了，因為他們必蒙憐憫。

馬太福音5:7

品格塑造
憐憫

年幼的小妹妹跟媽媽失散了，一時害怕亂跑，就衝出馬路，被車子撞倒，昏了過去。在之後的半小時裡，有許多途人經過，卻沒有人伸出援手幫助她。最後有一位老婆婆把她抱到安全的地方去，然後找警察來救她。後來，記者問經過的人為甚麼不理她，有的說自己匆匆走過，看不見她；有的說看見她，卻沒空幫忙；有的怕麻煩，裝作看不見就走開了。記者在新聞報道中感歎說："難道現在的人都沒有憐憫之心嗎？"

禱告

親愛的主耶穌，感謝你，因為神是愛。我想多多學習憐憫別人，不再自私。祈禱奉耶穌的名，阿們。

Blessed are the merciful, for they shall receive mercy.

Matthew 5:7

Character Builder
To Be Compassionate

A little girl panics when she is separated from her mom by a crowd. And she ends up being run down by a car. In the next half hour, many pass by but no one helps. Finally an old lady picks up the little girl, bringing her to a safe place and calling the police. A reporter gets curious and starts asking people questions. Their answers go: "I was in a rush;" "I didn't see her;" "I had more important things to do;" "It was too much trouble;" etc. This reporter laments, "How on earth have people become so heartless?"

Prayer

Dear Jesus, thank you for your love. I want to be full of compassion and not as selfish any more. Help me. In Your name, Amen.

想一想・做一做

1. 拉撒路天天在財主門口討飯，為甚麼財主不幫助他呢？

2. 如果你在路上看見這個品格故事中受傷的小妹妹，你會怎樣做？

3. 有甚麼原因令你缺少憐憫人的心？是沒空？是自私？記下原因，立志不再讓這些事情阻礙你憐憫別人。

A Life Lesson

1. Lazarus lies at the door of a rich man, begging for food. Why does the rich man do nothing?

2. If you were a passer-by and noticed that the little girl in the character story was hurt, what would you do?

3. Why do you sometimes show no compassion? Too busy? Too selfish? Write down the reasons. Tell yourself you will not let that happen again.

家長提示 / Tips for parents

都市人不能憐憫別人有很多原因，可能是怕別人欺騙自己，也可能是不想浪費自己的時間、金錢。總而言之，就是心裡太多計算。憐憫是神賜給人的特質，沒有憐憫，世界就變得醜陋和黑暗。別讓子女的心變得麻木，由今天起，就一起幫助別人，學習無私的付出吧！這樣才能感受到何謂"助人為快樂之本"。

Urban-city people have many excuses for incompassion – don't want to be swindled; don't want to waste time. All in all, they have become too calculating. God gives us the gift of compassion to bring light to this world of darkness. Do not ever let your children grow swamped by mercilessness. Instead, encourage them to step out of their comfort zone, bringing others blessings.

童來兒嬉 好撒瑪利亞人
Hoopla Whoopee Time *The Good Samaritan*

閱讀以下故事（路加福音10:25～37），並嘗試以戲劇形式表達重點。
Read Luke 10:25~37. Then act the drama out for better learning experience.

參考劇本 *Script Reference*

旁白：有一個猶太人要從耶路撒冷到耶利哥去，突然有強盜來打劫。強盜強行剝了猶太人的衣服，又打得他頭破血流，搶了他的財物就走了。不久，有一個祭司經過。

Narrator: A Jew is traveling from Jerusalem to Jericho. Suddenly, he is attacked by a robber. Beating him hard, the robber runs off with the man's clothes and all other belongings. And later, a priest walks by.

祭司（走到猶太人旁邊）：這個人受傷了！但我要回到聖殿去工作，不可以被他的血沾污我！（祭司從他旁邊走過，沒有幫他。）

Priest (walking up to the Jew): This man is bleeding! But I have to go to work in the temple, and I must not let his blood-stain make me unclean! (Priest walks off, not helping the Jew.)

旁白：過了不久，又有一個利未人經過，看見這個受傷的人。

Narrator: After a while, a Levite passes by, seeing the wounded man.

利未人：我可不想惹麻煩呢！（利未人快速地離開了。）

Levite: I don't want to get into trouble! (He quickly disappears.)

旁白：又過了不久，有一個撒瑪利亞人拖著驢子經過這裡，看見這個受傷的人，就憐憫他。

Narrator: Still more time is passed, a Samaritan comes near with his donkey. And seeing the man hurting, he has compassion on him.

撒瑪利亞人（扶起那人）：你傷得很重呢！不要怕，讓我來幫你吧！（撒瑪利亞人拿出油和酒倒在他的傷處。）

Samaritan (sitting the man up): You really are hurt badly! But don't be afraid; let me help you! (He begins to treat the wounds with oil and wine.)

旁白：撒瑪利亞人替受傷的猶太人止血，又用紗布包紮妥當，再扶他上驢子，帶他到旅店去照顧他。

Narrator: The Samaritan stops the bleeding, binds the wounds, sits the man on his donkey. And off they go to a resting place for further aid.

-完- -The End-

討論：像好撒瑪利亞人一樣幫助別人，有甚麼麻煩和困難的地方？

Discuss: What is so trouble or difficult to do to help a needy person as does the Good Samaritan?

撒該獲耶穌接納
Zacchaeus Is Accepted by Jesus

路加福音Luke
19:1~10

耶利哥城有個稅吏長撒該，他常欺壓別人，許多人不喜歡他。耶穌進城的時候，他很想見見耶穌，但是人很多，他的身材又矮小，怎麼都看不見。於是，撒該就跑到前面去，爬上了一棵桑樹。

耶穌往上一看，對他說：“撒該，快下來！今天我要住在你家裡。”

Zacchaeus was a chief tax collector in the City of Jericho. He was such an oppressor; no one liked him. When Jesus was entering the city, he wanted to see Jesus but there were too many people. Being a short man he couldn't see anything. So Zacchaeus ran ahead and climbed onto a sycamore-fig tree.

Jesus looked up and said to him, "Zacchaeus, come down! Today I must stay in your house."

撒該就趕快下來，歡歡喜喜地接待耶穌。眾人議論紛紛，但是耶穌接納和包容撒該。撒該以行動回應說：「主啊，我把財產的一半分給窮人，我騙了誰，就還他四倍。」

Zacchaeus came down at once and joyfully received Jesus. As the crowd tittle-tattled, Jesus accepted and embraced Zacchaeus. Zacchaeus said, "Lord, I give half of my wealth to the poor and if I have cheated any one, I will pay back four times the amount."

愛是凡事包容，凡事相信，凡事盼望，凡事忍耐。

哥林多前書13:7

品格塑造
包容

寶兒是我班裡的"搗蛋怪"，同學都不喜歡她，但是她很喜歡跟我聊天。我告訴媽媽："寶兒常跟我聊天，同學以為我跟她一夥，都不跟我玩了！"媽媽對我說："我跟寶兒媽媽談過，知道寶兒很孤單，想引人注意才這麼頑皮，我們可以多些關心她，多些包容她。"

媽媽教我寫心意卡給寶兒，勸她不要搗蛋，後來我才發現，原來寶兒也真的會乖呢！

禱告

親愛的主耶穌，感謝你寬大包容，求你賜我愛心，懂得關心和接納別人。祈禱奉耶穌的名，阿們。

113

Love bears all things, believes all things, hopes all things, endures all things.

1 Corinthians 13:7

Character Builder
To Be Tolerant

Bo is a mischief-maker in class; no one likes her, including me. But since Bo likes to chat with me, the other classmates think we are of the same kind, and they keep me at a distance. Mom tells me, "I talk with Bo and I know she is very lonely. She gets mischievous just to get attention. Maybe more people should care about her, give her another chance."

Mom helps me make cards for her, urging her to make positive changes. After a while, Bo becomes a likable person indeed!

Prayer

Dear Jesus, you are loving and kind. Make me accept and care for someone who is special to you. In Your name, Amen.

114

想—想・做—做

1. 撒該為了見見耶穌，他做了甚麼事？

2. 你學校裡有沒有像寶兒一樣搗蛋的同學？你喜歡跟她做朋友嗎？

3. 嘗試關心一些不受歡迎的同學，例如送贈心意卡。

A Life Lesson

1. In order to see Jesus, what does Zacchaeus do?

2. Is there someone like Bo in your class? How do you like to befriend this person?

3. Try to care for someone who is unpopular at school. E.g., make a gift card.

家長提示

我們都不是完美的人，假如你對人有偏見，就要想想自己也有很多缺點，同樣需要別人包容。與此同時，家長要多肯定子女的優點，讓他們也學習發掘別人的優點，假以時日，他們就不會那麼容易戴上"有色眼鏡"來看別人了。

Tips for Parents

We all are imperfect. Just as many flaws you find in others, they see more in you. As we learn to be more tolerant, we must also strive to affirm and approve. In due course, we would tend less to become critical and biased; rather, we would go for getting the best out of any person.

童來兒嬉 Hoopla Whoopee Time 尋找撒該大行動 Operation Scoop Out

圖中共有4個矮子撒該隱藏著，試把他們圈出來。

Circle out the not-so-tall Zacchaeus in the picture below. There are four such figures.

拉撒路復活
Lazarus Raised from the Dead

約翰福音John
11:1~6, 17~44

117

有 一天，拉撒路的姐姐馬利亞和馬大請人告訴耶穌，拉撒路病得很嚴重。耶穌聽了，說："這病不至於死，而是要使神得到榮耀。" 耶穌沒有立刻去，仍然在原來的地方往了兩天。後來，拉撒路死了，大家把他埋葬了。

One day, Lazarus' sisters Mary and Martha sent word to Jesus that Lazarus was very ill. When Jesus heard the news, he said, "This illness will not end in death, but that God may be glorified." However, Jesus did not go immediately, he stayed two days longer in ther place where he was. Lazarus died and the people buried him.

過了四天，耶穌來了。馬利亞非常傷心，忍受不了，痛哭起來，說：“如果你早點來，拉撒路就不會死了。”耶穌說：“他必會復活。”耶穌來到拉撒路的墳前，向父神禱告，然後大聲呼叫：“拉撒路，出來！”

Four days later, Jesus arrived. Mary was very sad and cried. She said, "If you had come earlier, Lazarus would not have died." Jesus answered, "He will live again." Jesus came to the tomb of Lazarus and prayed to God and then called out loudly, "Lazarus, come out!"

拉撒路就從墳墓裡出來了！他的手和腳還裹著布。耶穌對眾人說： "把布解開，讓他走！"

So, Lazarus came out of the tomb! His hands and feet were still wrapped in the grave clothes. Jesus told the people, "Take off the grave clothes and let him go!"

唯有堅忍到底的，必然得救。

馬太福音24:13

品格塑造
忍耐

兩位探險家沉船，流落荒島。偉仁問："怎會有這意外呢？"信堅回答："神一定會救我們。"他們用木搭房子暫住，禱告求神派船來救他們，卻沒有半點回應。偉仁破口大罵："難道神不知道我們快死在這裡嗎？為甚麼還不派人來呢？"信堅安慰他說："神自有計劃，我們只管忍耐禱告。"兩天後，房子失火，冒出大量濃煙，偉仁正要埋怨神，卻看見有船駛來，他們喜出望外，招手求救。後來船主跟他們說："我們看見濃煙，知道有人求救，才過來看看。"偉仁聽後立刻跪下感謝神。

禱告

親愛的主耶穌，感謝你愛我，求你教我學習忍耐等候的功課，明白你自有計劃。祈禱奉耶穌的名，阿們。

But the one who endures to the end will be saved.

Matthew 24:13

Character Builder
To Be Patient

Two men are stranded in an island; their ship has sunk. Andy complains, "How come this is happening to me?" Bobby replies reassuringly, "God will save us!" Later they build for themselves a wood hut, pray even more, yet no rescue arrives. Andy breaks into abuse, "Doesn't God care? Why isn't He sending us help?" Bobby tries to comfort him, "Be patient! God knows His plan; we keep on praying." Two days later, the hut is on fire and the smoke is thick. Just as Andy is about to denounce God, a rescue boat appears. The captain on the boat says, "We are here because we see the smoke." Hearing this, Andy falls on his knees praising God.

Prayer

Dear Jesus, thank you for your patient kind of love. Teach me the lesson of being patient with you, knowing you always have a plan. In Your name, Amen.

想一想・做一做

1. 為甚麼馬利亞會埋怨主耶穌？她這樣做對嗎？為甚麼？

2. 故事裡哪一個探險家比較懂得信靠神？為甚麼？

3. 有甚麼事情令你最不能忍耐等候？說出原因，並學習用禱告培養耐性。

A Life Lesson

1. Why is Mary complaining? Is it right that she does? Why?

2. In the shipwreck story, who has enduring faith? Why?

3. Name a few things that drive you restless. What are the reasons? How do you build a prayer life to foster forbearance?

家長提示

子女欠缺耐性，跟科技發達有關。因為現代人無論是溝通，或是尋找資料，只要連線上網，甚麼答案都一應俱全。他們越欠缺耐性，就越不能明白神的計劃，甚至以為用自己的方法就可以解決問題。嘗試多透過禱告來學習等候忍耐，讓子女慢慢認識神的作為，禱告切忌功利。

Tips for Parents

We run out of patience for a reason – technology has had us fooled. We tend to believe that immediate solution is available, just as the internet to search for any answers is in our grip. The fact is, without patience, we will fail to understand God's plan. What's worse, we rely on ourselves more. Let us train our children well in prayer business; no one should pray just to get what one wants.

童來兒嬉 禱告記錄表
Hoopla Whoopee Time *A Prayer Sheet*

請在空格上填寫，從而逐步認識神奇妙的作為。

Please fill in the blanks, and trace God's work of wonders.

禱告日期 *Date of Prayer*	代禱事項 *I Pray About...*	最新進展 *What's the Latest?*

十個患大痲瘋的人
Healing the Ten Men with Leprosy

路加福音Luke
17:11~19

耶穌經過撒瑪利亞和加利利的邊境，走進一個村莊。有十個患了大痲瘋的人迎面而來，遠遠站著，大聲說："主耶穌啊，可憐我們吧！"

耶穌就對他們說："你們去給祭司檢查一下吧。"他們就去了，還在路上的時候，身上的大痲瘋就全部好過來了！

Jesus was traveling along the border of Samaria and Galilee. As he was entering a village, ten men who had leprosy came towards him. They stood at a distance and shouted in a loud voice, "Lord Jesus, have pity on us!"

Jesus saw them and said, "Go and show yourselves to the priests." As they went on the way, the leprosy was cleansed and they were healed!

有個撒瑪利亞人回來，俯伏在地上，並且感謝耶穌。耶穌問道："得到醫治的不是十個人嗎？其餘九個在哪裡呢？再沒有一個人回來頌讚神嗎？"

A Samaritan came back and bowed on the ground to thank Jesus. Jesus asked, "Were not all ten healed? Where are the other nine? Are there no one else to give praise to God?"

內中有一個人見自己已經好了，就回來大聲頌讚神，在耶穌腳前把臉伏在地上感謝他。

路加福音17:15~16a

品格塑造 感恩

大鷹不小心掉進捕鳥人的網羅裡，農夫聽見牠淒厲的叫聲，就把牠放了。第二天，農夫耕種累了就脫下草帽，靠在舊屋牆壁休息睡著了。突然，那隻大鷹把農夫手上的草帽抓走，農夫醒來趕快去追。追了十多步，大鷹把草帽掉在地上，農夫撿起時，響起轟隆聲音，農夫回頭一看，那舊屋的牆壁忽然倒塌。至此，農夫和大鷹都感謝對方救了自己一命。

禱告

親愛的主耶穌，衷心感謝你每天賜恩給我，求你給我力量聽從你的教導，報答你的恩惠。祈禱奉耶穌的名，阿們。

Then one of them, when he saw that he was healed, turned back, praising God with a loud voice; and he fell on his face at Jesus' feet, giving him thanks.

Luke 17:15~16a

Character Builder
To Be Grateful

An eagle falls into the hunter's trap. A farmer hears its shrieks and sets it free. The next day after some hard work, the farmer takes off his straw hat and leans against the wall of an old shack to rest. He soon falls asleep. Suddenly, the eagle swoops down to take away the hat. The farmer is awakened and begins to chase the eagle. Only after a dozen paces does he hear a big bang from behind out of the wall tumbling. Indeed, both the man and the bird are grateful their lives are saved mutually.

Prayer

Dear Jesus, thank you for the wonderful daily gifts. Strengthen me to carry out your commands as a way of my repaying your love. In Your name, Amen.

想一想．做一做

1. 如果你是其中一個得醫治的痲瘋病人，你會回去感謝耶穌嗎？為甚麼？

2. 那隻大鷹如何報答農夫？

3. 為神給你恩典感謝祂；為曾恩待你的人，預備一份簡單的心意禮物，如公仔貼紙，然後送給他。

A Life Lesson

1. If you were one of the lepers who gets healed by Jesus, would you go back to the Lord to give thanks? Why?

2. What does the eagle do to repay the farmer?

3. Thank God for His great gifts; prepare for those who have been nice to you simple gifts such as stickers.

家長提示

教導子女成為感恩的人，就要學習即時感恩。不要把早上值得感恩的事留待晚上才數算，甚至等到年終感恩會時才回想。從日常生活做起，例如：教導子女收到禮物，或得到別人幫助，都要即時說謝謝。日子有功，子女就容易學會凡事謝恩。

Tips for Parents

To teach your children to be grateful is to teach them to repay without delay. Don't wait until the evening to return a blessing received in the morning. Start with daily encounters: Say thank you instantly when a gift or an offer of help is in the lap. More practices will later form a habit.

童來兒嬉 我的禮物
Hoopla Whoopee Time *My Gift*

請記下恩人名字，並簡述所施恩惠。然後，製作一張謝卡，送給其中一位。

Name those to whom you owe big thanks, and briefly describe what happens. Then, make a card to give to one of them.

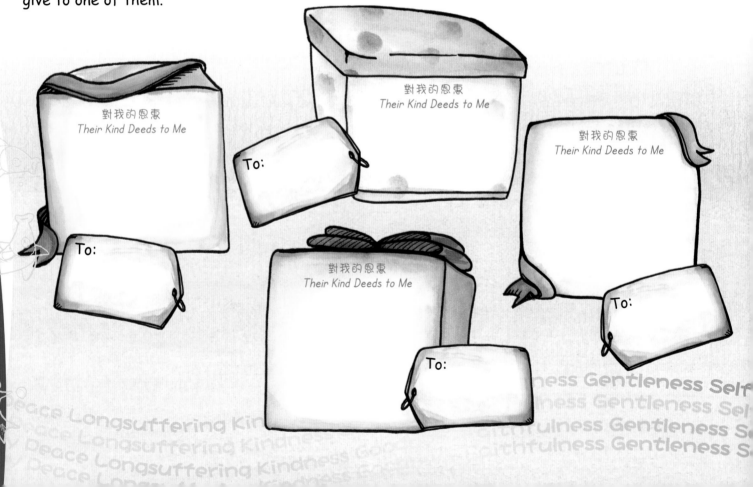

對我的恩惠
Their Kind Deeds to Me

To:

對我的恩惠
Their Kind Deeds to Me

對我的恩惠
Their Kind Deeds to Me

To:

對我的恩惠
Their Kind Deeds to Me

To:

To:

奉獻香膏的女人
The Woman with the Ointment

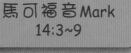

馬可福音Mark
14:3~9

耶穌在一個人的家裡作客。有個女人，拿了一瓶珍貴的香膏過來，倒在耶穌的頭上。立時，整個房子充滿了芬芳的香氣。

門徒看見，就很生氣，說："為甚麼這樣浪費呢？如果把這香膏賣了，可以換成很多的錢，用來幫助窮人！"

Jesus was a guest at the home of a man. A woman came with a jar of expensive ointment and poured it on Jesus' head. The whole house was filled with beautiful fragrance.

When Jesus' disciples saw this, they were indignant and said, "Why this waste? This ointment could be sold for a high price and the money used for the poor."

耶穌卻說："她為我做的是一件美事，她預先用香膏膏抹我，是為了我的安葬。常常有窮人跟你們在一起，你們要行善隨時都可以，但你們不是常常有我。"

Jesus said, "She has done a beautiful thing for me. She poured this ointment on me to prepare me for my burial. You will always have the poor with you and you can help them at any time, but you will not always have me."

背一背

我實在告訴你們，這福音無論傳到世界上甚麼地方，這女人所作的都要傳講，來記念她。

馬太福音26:13

品格塑造
體貼

一個富商看見很多窮孩子流連街上，就想興建遊樂場，免費讓他們遊玩。他對建築師說出這構思，建築師就說："我相信那些窮孩子將來一定玩得很開心，但是他們真的最需要這些嗎？"富商再三細想，就決定先興建學校和圖書館，因為學習比遊玩重要。

禱告

親愛的耶穌，感謝你教導我，了解別人需要是重要的。祈禱奉耶穌的名，阿們。

Truly, I say to you, wherever this gospel is proclaimed in the whole world, what she has done will also be told in memory of her.

Matthew 26:13

Character Builder
To Be Considerate

A businessman wants to build a playground for the poor children so they don't have to roam the street. His friend asks him, "The kids may have a good time playing. But is that what they need the most?" The businessman ponders and changes his mind. He builds a school with a big library instead.

Prayer

Dear Jesus, thank you for teaching me about the needs of others. In Your name, Amen.

想一想・做一做

1. 那位奉獻香膏的女人和門徒分別重視甚麼？

2. 富商為窮孩子興建遊樂場有甚麼問題？他首先考慮的是甚麼？

3. 說出一次你助人的經歷。那次你是以別人的需要出發嗎？

A Life Lesson

1. How do the woman and the disciples differ in what they see as important?

2. Is it any wrong that the businessman wants to build a playground? What is he first preoccupied with?

3. Share the last time you helped a person. Did you do it out of consideration?

家長提示　Tips for Parents

很多家長以為子女需要的是物質供應，其實他們需要的很多都是非物質的，包括愛心、包容和諒解等。嘗試和子女一起參與義工活動，例如：幫助獨居老人清潔家居，到醫院探望患病的小朋友，讓他們有機會多體貼別人的需要，這對他們的成長很有幫助。

Many parents make the mistake of supplying their children with an abundance of material goods. In fact, what these children need the most is beyond material affluence – compassion, forgiveness, understanding. Try and work as volunteers with your kids – helping the elderly who live alone to clean up, or to visit the sick in a children's hospital. More of these kind deeds means more into caring for what people really need.

童來兒嬉 我的香膏瓶
Hoopla Whoopee Time *My Ointment Jar*

在香膏瓶內寫下一些你願意關心別人的行動，
然後逐一實行出來。

List out in the jar a few kind things you want to do.
Then act on them.

耶穌被釘十架
Jesus Nailed on the Cross

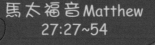

馬太福音Matthew
27:27~54

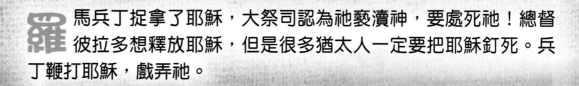

羅馬兵丁捉拿了耶穌，大祭司認為祂褻瀆神，要處死祂！總督彼拉多想釋放耶穌，但是很多猶太人一定要把耶穌釘死。兵丁鞭打耶穌，戲弄祂。

The Roman soldiers came to arrest Jesus. The high priest said that he had spoken blasphemy and he should die! Pilate wanted to release him. But the Jews would rather have Jesus crucified. The soldiers whipped Jesus and mocked him.

兵丁用荊棘編成冠冕戴在耶穌頭上，又把耶穌釘在十字架上。下午三時，遍地黑暗。耶穌大聲呼叫，氣就斷了。

The soldiers made a crown out of thorns and put it on Jesus' head. They then nailed Jesus on a cross. At three o'clock in the afternoon, the whole earth was in darkness. Jesus cried out loudly and breathed his last.

忽然，地面震動，石頭崩裂，墳墓都打開了。百夫長和兵丁都很害怕，說："這真是神的兒子！"

Suddenly, the earth shook and the rocks split. Even the tombs broke open. The centurion and the soldiers were frightened and said, "This really is the Son of God!"

神愛世人，甚至把他的獨生子賜給他們，叫一切信他的，不至滅亡，反得永生。

約翰福音3:16

品格塑造
無私奉獻

媽媽跟洛宜分享了《快樂小王子》的故事，洛宜明白"助人是快樂之本"，就立志要做"快樂公主"，學習為別人犧牲。她在路上看見乞丐又冷又餓，就把買零食的錢給他；她遇見老婆婆打著冷顫拾廢紙皮，就把自己心愛的一對手套給她。回到家中，她高興地對媽媽說："原來幫助別人，真是很喜樂。我以後也要做快樂公主，樂意把自己的東西奉獻給人。"

禱告

親愛的 主耶穌，感謝你為我的罪被釘十架，使我與神和好，我也要學習你的榜樣，使別人都認識你。祈禱奉耶穌的名，阿們。

For God so loved the world, that he gave his only Son, that whoever believes in him should not perish but have eternal life.

John 3:16

Character Builder
To Be Self-Giving

Rosy loves the story her mom tells, and she wants to be like the Happy Prince in the book, who will sacrifice himself to make others happy. In fact, Rosy is determined to be the Happy Princess. She gives her allowance to mom, buying food for the homeless; she throws in her mitten so that the bare hands of an old small lady who lives on picking scrap papers won't quiver in the cold. "It feels good to be able to help others. I want to be the Happy Princess all my life," she asserts.

Prayer

Dear Jesus, you died on the cross to take away my sin, so that I can be right with Father God. Help me to tell others of you. In Your name, Amen.

想一想・做一做

1. 耶穌被釘十架，祂為人犧牲了甚麼？

2. 你認為洛宜懂得無私奉獻的道理嗎？為甚麼？

3. 有誰曾為你奉獻自己？他／她做了甚麼事？你會怎樣報答他／她？

A Life Lesson

1. What does Jesus sacrifice for the mankind when he is hung on the cross?

2. Do you think Rosy understands the meaning of self-giving? Why?

3. Who has sacrificed for you? What has this person done? How are you going to repay him/her?

家長提示　Tips for Parents

無私奉獻可以很偉大，像耶穌為罪人被釘十架。然而家長可以從小事開始教導子女學會奉獻，就像窮寡婦把養生的兩個小錢奉獻給神。如果子女也願意為了更重要的事而放棄心愛的東西，他們就漸漸明白耶穌的奉獻精神了。當然，家長也要跟子女一起學習才有效呢！

Self-giving sacrifices can be quite magnificent, as Jesus died on the cross. Yet, parents can teach their children to make humble ones at a young age, like what the poor widow did with her two copper coins. If our children become willing to surrender what they like in exchange for what matters to God, then they surely have mastered the lesson of self-giving. In this parents must make model for their children.

童來兒嬉 實踐無私奉獻
Hoopla Whoopee Time Self-giving to Become

寫出三樣實踐 "無私奉獻" 的行動，並在未來一個月內逐一實踐。

Take a month to put three self-giving deeds listed below into action.

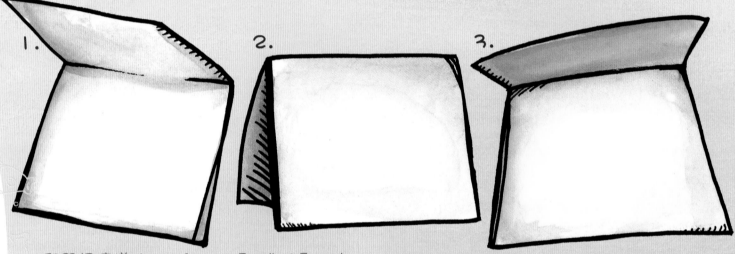

1.

2.

3.

學習好榜樣 Learn from an Excellent Example

家長跟子女一起觀賞謝婉雯醫生及其他醫護人員在沙士期間犧牲生命的見證，然後一起討論以下問題：

First watch a video clip about Dr Tse Yuen Man, who died with a handful of health professionals while treating patients, trying to protect them from the assault of the SARS disease. Then, discuss:

如果我是謝婉雯醫生，我會冒生命危險去救人嗎？

If I were Dr Tse, would I sacrifice myself to save others?

見證連結 Go here for the video: http://www.youtube.com/watch?v=nQYHaySMqVA

耶穌復活

The Resurrection of Jesus

路加福音Luke
24:1~9, 36~43

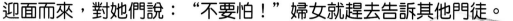

被釘十字架的耶穌第三天復活了！

禮拜天大清早，婦女帶著香料來到墳墓那裡，卻找不著耶穌的身體。耶穌向她們迎面而來，對她們說：＂不要怕！＂婦女就趕去告訴其他門徒。

On the third day after Jesus was crucified, he had risen!

Early on Sunday morning, the women brought spices to the tomb but could not find Jesus' body. Jesus came towards them and said, "Do not fear!" The women hurried to tell the other disciples.

門徒和眾人在耶路撒冷聚集。耶穌忽然站在他們當中，說：“願你們平安！”他們非常害怕，以為看見了鬼靈。耶穌把手和腳給他們看，他們歡喜得不敢相信。耶穌還在他們的面前吃了一片燒魚。

The apostles and the other disciples were meeting in Jerusalem. Jesus suddenly appeared in their midst and said, "Peace be with you!" They were afraid, thinking that they were seeing a ghost. Jesus showed them his hands and feet. They still couldn't believe it because of joy. Jesus ate a piece of roasted fish in front of them.

耶穌在提比里亞海邊再次向門徒顯現。耶穌說："你們來，吃早飯吧！" 門徒沒有一個人問祂是誰，因為知道祂是主。

Jesus appeared to the disciples again beside the Sea of Tiberias. Jesus said, "Come and have breakfast." The disciples did not ask who he was, as they knew that he was the Lord.

背一背

所有信靠他的人，必不致失望。

羅馬書10:11

品格塑造
信靠

遠足前，爸爸再三吩咐兒子："要是失散了，你一定要留在原地，爸爸一定來找你。"遠足當日，兒子興奮地往前跑，竟在岔路口跟爸爸失散，哭著叫爸爸。一個陌生男人跑過來哄他說："你爸爸叫我來帶你到附近的涼亭去找他。"小兒子想起爸爸的吩咐，就說："爸爸叫我在這裡等，他十分可靠，一定會自己來找我的。"就在這時，爸爸從遠處跑來，那人害怕起來就走了。

禱告

親愛的主耶穌，感謝你為我釘在十架上，又從死裡復活，使我們知道你是最值得信靠的。祈禱奉耶穌的名，阿們。

159

Everyone who believes in him will not be put to shame.

Romans 10:11

Character Builder
To Be Trusting

A father goes hiking with his son. Before setting off, the father reminds the son, "If we are separated, do not wander off. I definitely will come back and look for you." On the way, the son happily runs ahead and is separated from the father. His tearful eyes look for the father. However, a stranger comes towards him and says, "Your father told me to take you to the nearby pavilion." But the son remembers his father's instructions and says, "My father told me to wait for him here and I trust that he will come looking for me himself." Just then, his father runs forward from afar and the stranger quickly disappears.

Prayer

Dear Jesus, thank you for you died on the cross and rose from the dead for me. Make me realize that you are the most trustworthy. In Your name, Amen.

想一想・做一做

1. 如果你是其中一位門徒，你會相信耶穌真的復活了嗎？為甚麼？

2. 故事中的兒子為甚麼沒跟從陌生人？

3. 說出可靠的人的兩個條件？你會如何使自己有這些條件。

A Life Lesson

1. If you were one of the disciples, would you believe that Jesus had risen from the dead? Why?

2. In the character story, why didn't the son follow the stranger?

3. What makes a person trustworthy? Name two qualities, and how do you develop such qualities?

家長提示

信靠的基礎是愛，所以跟子女培養互動而友愛的關係是很要緊的，"不輕易許下諾言" 和 "守祕密" 是培養這種關係的竅門。前者使你不易失去子女信任的一票，後者令子女直接認為你是可信靠的。

Tips for Parents

Love is the basis of trust, so it is important to build up a mutual loving relationship with the children. Two of the keys in building this relationship are "Never to make a promise lightly" and "Do keep a secret". The former prevents you from losing the child's confidence; the latter signals to the child that you can be trusted.

童來兒嬉 信靠的懷抱
Hoopla Whoopee Time *Embrace of Trust*

子女背向家長直立，雙腳不許彎曲，勿向後看，然後挨倒向家長，家長要接住子女。跟著，請子女說出感受。（這遊戲是讓子女明白，信任別人要靠雙方關係和勇氣。）

The child stands with his back towards the parent. Without looking back, the child leans back knees straight towards the parent until the parent catches the child. After the game, the child shares the feeling. (Purpose: Teach children that relationship and courage are the keys to trusting in others.)

傳揚福音

Proclaiming the Gospel

使徒行傳Acts
1:6~11

耶穌帶門徒到加利利的一座山上，對他們說：「聖靈要降臨在你們身上，你們就必領受能力，並且，你們要在全地上作我的見證人。」之後，有一朵雲彩把祂接走了。

Jesus led the disciples to a mountain in Galilee and said to them, "The Holy Spirit will come upon you and you will receive power. You will be my witnesses to the ends of the earth." Then Jesus was taken up into heaven in a cloud.

165

耶穌往上升的時候，大家都定睛望天。忽然，有兩個穿著白衣的人，告訴他們耶穌怎樣升天，祂還要怎樣回來。

The disciples were looking up into the sky when Jesus was being taken up into heaven. Suddenly two men dressed in white appeared and said to them, "In the same way he will come back."

品格塑造 忠於所託

巴黎有座又大又美麗的教堂，可是，裡面放了一尊殘破的耶穌銅像，銅像有很多傷痕，而且沒有雙手。人近前來看時，發現下面有個牌子寫著："你們就是我的手"。

耶穌用釘痕的手拯救我們，醫治我們的心靈，赦免我們的罪。我們這些信耶穌的人，就是耶穌的手，必須忠於所託，肩負責任向人傳福音，作見證，帶領別人相信主耶穌。

禱告

親愛的天父，感謝你差派耶穌來傳講福音，求你給我力量忠心完成你吩咐我做的事，將耶穌的事蹟告訴別人。祈禱奉耶穌的名，阿們。

167

But you will receive power when the Holy Spirit has come upon you, and you will be my witnesses in Jerusalem and in all Judea and Samaria, and to the end of the earth.

Acts 1:8

Character Builder
To Be Dedicated

There is a big and beautiful cathedral in Paris, but inside there is a broken bronze statue of Christ. The statue has many scratches and has no hands. When people stand closer they can see a plaque on which was written, "You are my hands."

Jesus' hands were pierced to rescue us and heal our hearts. He forgives our sins. We who believe in Jesus are his hands and carry the great commission: To preach the gospel and make disciples.

Prayer

Dear Father God, thank you for rising from the dead and sending the Holy Spirit to be with me, giving me the strength to complete the commission you gave me - telling people about Jesus. In Jesus' name, Amen.

想一想・做一做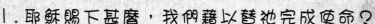

1. 耶穌賜下甚麼，我們藉以替祂完成使命？

2. 耶穌用釘痕的手做了甚麼事情？

3. 耶穌吩咐我們要傳福音給別人聽，那麼你想向誰傳福音？

A Life Lesson

1. What did Jesus give us to complete the great commission for him?

2. What did the pierced hands of Jesus do?

3. Jesus tells us to share the gospel with others, so who would you talk to?

家長提示　Tips for Parents

培養子女忠於所託可以由小任務開始，例如收拾玩具、擺放筷子等。子女做小任務時要給予提示和讚賞，但是切忌每次都給予物質的獎勵。

To cultivate a sense of dedication in a child, you can start from small tasks, such as tidying up toys or setting the table. Give some promptings and encouragements, but avoid giving material prizes every time.

童來兒嬉 小任務 · 大責任
Hoopla Whoopee Time *Small Tasks, Big Mission*

下圖的小朋友忙著做不同的事情，其實這是媽媽交給他們的責任，
你有沒有幫忙做這些任務？如果你曾完成哪些任務，請把哪位小朋友
附近的圓圈填上顏色，然後說出完成任務的感受。

The children in the picture are busy doing different chores. These are all given by the mother.
Have you helped in these tasks? If so, then color in the circle near the children doing that task
and tell about how you felt when you completed your chores.

五旬節聖靈降臨

The Holy Spirit Comes at Pentecost

使徒行傳Acts
2:1~4, 37~42

五旬節時，門徒聚集禱告。忽然，有一陣好像強風吹過的聲音，從天上而來，充滿了他們的房子，又出現火焰般的舌頭，分別落在他們各人身上。

At Pentecost, the disciples met together to pray. Suddenly a sound like that of a strong wind came from heaven and filled the whole house. What seemed like tongues of fire appeared and separately came to rest on them.

聖靈充滿他們了！按著聖靈所賜的能力，他們說起另外一種語言。那時，有很多人從世界各地來到耶路撒冷，彼得放膽勸勉他們要悔改信主，領受聖靈，那天，有三千人洗禮，加入教會。

They were filled with the Holy Spirit! By the power of the Holy Spirit, they began to speak in different languages. At that time, there were many people from different countries in Jerusalem. Peter boldly urged them to repent and receive the Holy Spirit. Three thousand were baptised and joined the church.

背一背

你們要靠主的大能大力，在他裡面剛強。

品格塑造
勇敢

三位小朋友正在
爭論誰最大膽。

伯志高聲說："我每次考試都作弊，就算
有老師在場，我也不怕，所以我最大膽！"仲
明自誇地說："我不但每次考試都作弊，而且
每次小測、默書都作弊，就算有兩位老師在場，
我也不怕，你們才不夠我大膽！"季文一臉正氣
地告訴他們："你們作弊是不對的！我不夠膽作
弊，但是你們如果不改過，我可夠膽把你們的
惡行告訴老師！"

你說這三位小朋友，誰最有膽量？我們
以為不怕危險就是勇敢，但事實
上堅持做對的事，才是勇
敢呢！

禱告

親愛的天父，感謝你賜
下聖靈，讓我可以靠聖靈
勇敢去做你喜歡我去做的
事。祈禱奉耶穌的名，
阿們。

175

Be Strong in the Lord and in the strength of his might.

Ephesians 6:10

Character Builder
To Be Brave

Three friends are debating who is the bravest.

Patrick says, "I cheat in every exam, even when the teacher is there, I ain't afraid. So I must be the bravest." Ming boastfully says, "I cheat not only in the exams, but also in every test. Even when there are two teachers, I ain't afraid. You are not as brave as me!" Man solemnly tells both, "You are wrong to cheat! I dare not cheat, but if you do not correct your way, I dare to report your bad conducts to the teachers!"

Who do you think is the bravest of the three? We think that being brave means doing dangerous things without fear, but actually being brave means doing the right thing according to the truth.

Prayer

Dear *Father God*, thank you for giving the Holy Spirit so that I can do the things that please you by relying on the Spirit. Please give me the brave to live the truth. In Jesus' name, Amen

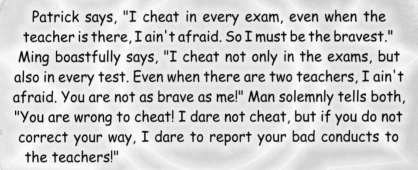

想一想．做一做

1. 門徒為甚麼勇敢傳福音不怕被捕？

2. 故事中三位小朋友的膽量有甚麼不同？

3. 講一件你勇敢堅持做對的事。

A Life Lesson

1. Why do the disciples bravely spread the gospel at the risk of being imprisoned?

2. What are the differences between the courage of the three friends?

3. Share an event in which you show the courage to do what is right.

家長提示

所謂"知恥近乎勇"，真正的勇敢並非單指敢於做危險的事，而是知羞恥，明對錯，堅持做對的事。要從小培養子女討神喜悅的特質，才能栽培他們成為真正勇敢的人！

Tips for Parents

To be bold comes from knowing shame. Real boldness is not about having the guts to do dangerous things. Rather, it is about knowing what is right and wrong and what is shameful, so that you can stick with what is right. We need to develop the children's character to please God starting from a young age, so that they can grow up to be truly courage.

童來兒嬉 聖靈果子在哪裡？
Hoopla Whoopee Time *Where is the Fruit of the Spirit?*

細心閱讀加拉太書5:22~23節，然後從下面的大樹上找回聖靈果子，並填上美麗的顏色。

Read Galatians 5:22~23 carefully, then find and color in the fruit of the Spirit from the tree below.

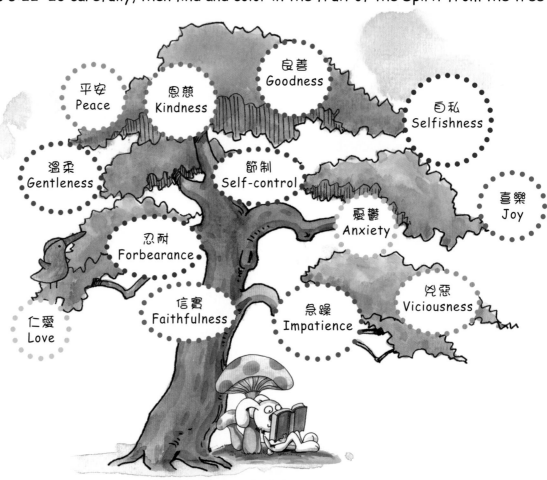

得人如得魚
Fishers of Men

使徒行傳Acts
2:44~3:10

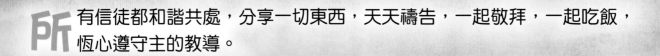

所 有信徒都和諧共處，分享一切東西，天天禱告，一起敬拜，一起吃飯，恆心遵守主的教導。

The disciples gathered together peacefully and shared everything. They prayed daily, broke bread and shared meals together, obediently following the teaching of the Lord.

有一個天生的跛子，天天被人抬到聖殿門口向人討飯。彼得對他說：「金銀我都沒有，我奉拿撒勒人耶穌基督的名，吩咐你起來行走！」他就跳起來，一邊走一邊讚美神，眾人看見都驚訝不已。

One day a man who was crippled from birth was being brought to the temple gate, where he begged for food every day. Peter said to him, "Gold and silver I do not have, but in the Name of Jesus of Nazareth I command you to walk!" He jumped up and began to walk, praising God. Everyone who saw this was amazed.

背一背

你們中間哪一個人，兒子向他要餅，反給他石頭；要魚，反給他蛇呢？

馬太福音7:9~10

品格塑造
體貼

1936至1939

年西班牙內戰期間，救援人員丹·威斯特從美國向交戰雙方的孩子分送奶粉。物資送完，飢餓的孩子還有很多，他就想："如果這些人家裡有母牛，就不用靠人養自己的孩子那麼丟臉了。"

於是，他創辦了國際小母牛，並在1944年首次送出18頭幼牛到波多黎各，又在1947年透過聯合國給中國首次送贈550頭乳牛。此後，這組織向超過125個國家送贈牲畜，受惠的貧困家庭超過1200萬戶。

禱告

親愛的天父，感謝你使跛子走路，求你也使我懂得體貼別人的需要，好為耶穌基督作見證。祈禱奉耶穌的名，阿們。

Or which one of you, if his son asks him for bread, will give him a stone? Or if he asks for a fish, will give him a serpent?

Matthew 7:9~10

Character Builder
To Be Considerate

Dan West serves as a relief worker during the Spanish Civil War (1936-1939). Every day he hands out powdered milk to children on both sides of the conflict. When the supply runs out, but the line of hungry children does not, he reasons, "If the families had dairy cows, they could spare the indignity of depending on others to feed their children."

So he helps found Heifer International, and in 1944 the first shipment of 18 heifers goes to Puerto Rico. In 1947, China receives its first shipment of 550 dairy cows through the UN. Since then, Heifer International has provided income source and training to more than 12 million poor families in over 125 countries.

Prayer

Dear *Father God*, thank you for healing the lame man. Make me an understanding person, sensitive to others' needs, bearing witness for Christ. In Jesus' name, Amen.

184

想一想．做一做

1. 跛子需要的是錢還是能走路的腳？

2. 國際小母牛送牛不送牛奶的做法有何好處？

3. 你需要的是錢，還是學識？你會怎樣增加你的學識？

A Life Lesson

1. What does the lame beggar really need – money or a pair of legs that walk?

2. Heifer International donates cows but not milk. What is the advantage of that?

3. Must you become a man of great wealth or of great learning? How do you increase your knowledge?

家長提示　Tips for Parents

真正的體貼，是家長明白子女需要的是照顧自己的能力，不是你的照顧。家長過分呵護子女，以致他們自理能力不足。家長可以從小事開始訓練他們，包括：收拾床舖、綁鞋帶、洗臉、擦牙，只要他們有能力做又不危險的都盡量讓他們自己做。你只是從旁指導，但千萬別見他們笨手笨腳就急著去幫，否則沒有你，他們就不懂做人了。

To be considerate, parents must understand what children need in the long haul is their own ability to self-care, not the parents'. Overprotection often deprives children of their capacity to self-care. Parents would be wise to train their children to make the bed, tie shoestrings, wash the face and brush the teeth, or do any competent things which do not put them in danger. Take a coach's role, instead; suppress the urge to interfere at any blunders, or else the children will never grow.

童來兒嬉 自摺和平鴿
Hoopla Whoopee Time *Make Your Own Folds*

子女自行依指示摺出和平鴿，家長可解釋或糾正，但千萬不要出手！

Fold a paper pigeon following the given hints. Parents can explain or correct, but not lay a finger!

1. 取一張正方形紙，向上對摺，再張開；
2. 向右對摺；
3. 沿虛線向右摺；
4. 沿虛線向左摺；
5. 張開最上頁的三角形，向下對摺；
6. 沿虛線向上摺出雙翼；
7. 在左邊的尖端上摺一下再摺回來；
8. 沿摺痕向內屈出嘴巴；
9. 畫上眼睛。

1. Fold in half to make a crease and fold back.
2. Fold in half.
3. Fold in the dotted line.
4. Fold in the dotted line.
5. Fold in half.
6. Fold in the dotted line. Back is the same too.
7. Fold to make a crease and fold back.
8. Fold inside and make a mouth.
9. Draw eyes to finish.

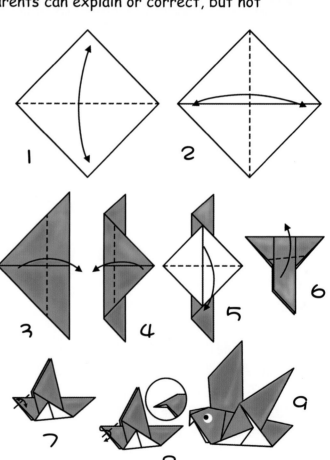

掃羅的奇遇
Saul's Experience

使徒行傳 Acts
9:1~19

掃羅迫害教會，時常發出恐嚇的話。他正在路上的時候，忽然，有光從天上向他四面照射過來！他就倒在地上。

耶穌問掃羅為甚麼迫害祂，掃羅從地上爬起來，張開眼睛，卻甚麼都看不見。三天之久，他不吃，也不喝，反省自己的過錯，並且悔改。

Saul persecuted the church and spoke out murderous threats. While he was on the road, a bright light from heaven suddenly flashed around him! He fell to the ground.

Jesus asked Saul, "Why do you persecute me?" Saul got up from the ground and opened his eyes, but he couldn't see. He did not eat or drink, but reflect and repent for three days.

亞拿尼亞為掃羅禱告，掃羅就能看見了。於是，掃羅受洗，聖靈充滿他，他大有能力傳講神的道，見證耶穌是神的兒子。

Ananias prayed for Saul and he could see again. So Saul was baptised and was filled with the Holy Spirit. He preached the word of God with power and testified that Jesus was the Son of God.

應當結出果子來,與悔改的心相稱。

路加福音3:8a

品格塑造
知錯能改

永光愛捉弄人,常常伸出腳來絆倒同學。雖然大家都討厭這種行為,永光卻以此為樂。有一次,他照樣伸出腳來,怎料有一位同學走過來,踏在他的足踝上,他痛得又叫又哭,結果要送進醫院。他第一次住在醫院裡,晚上怕黑,不敢上廁所,幸好鄰床的大哥哥主動幫助他。大哥哥問他為甚麼受傷,永光說出原因。大哥哥提醒他要愛護別人,要常常反省自己的錯誤。永光看見大哥哥樂於助人,得到眾人喜愛,開始明白自己的錯誤。

禱告

親愛的天父,感謝你讓我能夠學習反省,並給我機會改正過錯,求你賜我智慧,建立更美好的品格。祈禱奉耶穌的名,阿們。

I **Bear** fruits in keeping with repentance.

Luke 3:8a

Character Builder
To Be Repentant

Wing likes to play tricks on other people. He often puts out his foot to trip up his fellow students. Although everyone resents this behavior, he enjoys doing this all the more. Once, he puts out his foot again but the student who walks by steps on his foot. Wing cries out in pain and has to be sent to hospital. It is his first time in the hospital. At night he is afraid of the dark and dare not go to the toilet. Fortunately a young man in the next bed helps him. He asks Wing why he is injured. Wing tells him the reason. The young man reminds him to care for other people and to reflect on his own mistakes often. Wing sees that the young man is happy to help people and is well liked. He begins to realize his own mistakes.

Prayer

Dear Father God, thank you for teaching me to reflect on myself and for giving me a chance to correct my fault. Please give me the wisdom to build a better character. In Jesus' name, Amen.

想一想．做一做

1. 為甚麼耶穌要使掃羅三天不能看見東西？

2. 永光因作弄別人而受傷，對他來說是好事還是壞事？為甚麼？

3. 你最近有沒有做錯事？試細心想想錯在哪裡？並告訴父母如何改過。

A Life Lesson

1. Why does Jesus make Saul blind for three days?

2. Wing is injured because he is trying to trick others. Is going to the hospital a good thing or a bad thing for him? Why?

3. Have you done anything wrong recently? Think about what you have done wrong and tell your parents how you would correct your fault.

家長提示　Tips for Parents

曾子"吾日三省吾身"的做法，對教導今天的兒童有十分重要的作用。"吾日三省吾身"意指每天不斷藉著反省來檢查自己有沒有改進的地方。只是知易行難，特別是年幼的子女，如何能教導他們知錯能改？每天祈禱和讀聖經就是最好的方法。人靠著耶穌才能學會反省，"不是倚靠權勢，不是倚靠能力，而是倚靠神的靈。"（撒迦利亞書4:6）

A Confucian influence imparts: "reflect on self three times a day". This teaching has great importance in modern child education. Its meaning is to self-inspect daily to see if there is room for improvement. However, it is easier said than done, especially for young children. How do you teach them to be repentant? Daily reading of the Bible and prayer is a good method. We can self-reflect only by relying on Jesus. "Not by might, nor by power, but by my Spirit." (Zechariah 4:6)

童來兒嬉 猜一猜，像不像？
Hoopla Whoopee Time *Blind Guess*

預備幾樣形狀、體積、質料都不同的物件（要安全的），然後請子女閉起雙眼，家長選取一件物品出來，給子女觸摸，然後說出物品的名稱。如果有多名子女參與，可互相討論才說出答案。猜中的獲獎糖果，猜不中的則送貼紙。

遊戲後，請子女說出＂看不見＂的感受，然後引導他們思想沒有自我反省的人，就像盲人摸東西一樣，只堅持自己所＂看見＂的，不會聽別人的意見，結果只會使自己失去學習的機會。

Prepare a few items of different shapes, sizes and materials (which are safe) and then tell the children to close their eyes. Parents take out an item and give it to the children to feel. They have to tell what the item is. If there are many children, they can discuss together before answering. A correct answer may be rewarded with a candy and a wrong answer with a sticker as encouragement.

After the game, ask the children how it feels not to be able to see. Then lead them to think about a person who does not self-reflect is like a blind person who can only feel and does not listen to other people's ideas. He will only fail to learn.

天使營救彼得
Peter Was Saved by the Angel

使徒行傳Acts
12:1~18

彼得因為傳福音，被羅馬政府捉拿了，遭兩條鎖鏈鎖住，旁邊還有兩個兵丁把守。彼得因為信靠神，睡著了，忽然天使出現，拍拍彼得的肋旁，鎖鏈就脫落了。彼得跟著天使，來到通往城裡的鐵門，那門自動打開了。

Because of his preaching of the Word, Peter was imprisoned by the Roman government. He was bound with two chains and two Roman soldiers kept watch beside him. Because Peter trusted God, he fell asleep. Suddenly an angel appeared, struck Peter on the side and his chains fell off. Peter followed the angel and came to the iron gate which led to the city and the gate opened by itself.

彼得到眾人那裡去，他們正在禱告，看見彼得時，都驚訝得不敢相信。天亮的時候，士兵非常慌亂，不知道彼得哪裡去了，在全城搜索，可是怎樣也找不到。

Peter went to where the disciples were meeting. They were praying and when they saw Peter, they were too astonished to believe. In the morning, the soldiers were in turmoil. They didn't know where Peter had gone. They searched the whole city and couldn't find him.

背一背 你們得救是靠著恩典，藉著信心。這不是出於自己，而是神所賜的。

以弗所書2:8

品格塑造 信靠

一位宣教士到非洲部落宣教，並為當地的土著翻譯聖經。當他正為怎樣翻譯"信心"這個詞而苦惱時，他看到一個土著工作後，整個人安坐在一張躺椅上，露出非常舒服、放鬆的神情。宣教士興奮地大叫："這就是'信心'啊！"他最後用"躺坐"這個詞翻譯"信心"，表達聖經裡信心所含"交託"、"信靠"的意思。

禱告

親愛的天父，感謝你每天都看顧我，我願學習更加信靠你。祈禱奉耶穌的名，阿們。

For by grace you have been saved through faith. And this is not your own doing, it is the gift of God.

Ephesians 2:8

Character Builder
To Be Trusting

A missionary goes to Africa, works in a tribe and learns to translate the Bible into the local dialect. Once he is distressed at failing to find a term for "faith." Then he notices a tribesman who sinks into a reclining seat after a long hard day, displaying a most comfy posture. The translator yells, "That's it!" And he decides to use the term "slump" for "faith," indicating biblical faith as a form of "leaning on", "trusting".

Prayer

*Dear **Father God**, thank you for watching over me every day. Teach me to rely on you totally. In Jesus' name, Amen.*

想一想・做一做

1. 為甚麼彼得坐牢可以安然睡著？

2. 聖經裡的信心包含甚麼意思？

3. 寫下（或以圖畫表達）甚麼叫信靠天父。

A Life Lesson

1. How come Peter sleeps soundly when in jail?

2. What is the meaning of faith in the Bible?

3. Write or draw to express the meaning of having faith in God.

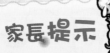

家長提示

要子女學習信靠神，不能單靠講故事和背經文，更重要的是以身作則，讓子女感到家長是可信任的，他們才能學會信靠天父。

Tips for parents

You cannot teach children trusting in God just by telling stories or memorizing Scripture. It is more important to model an example, so that the children can feel that they can experience trustworthiness from parents. Then they will learn to trust in our Father in Heaven.

童來兒嬉 信心領航
Hoopla Whoopee Time *Faith Navigates*

請子女閉上雙眼，不准偷看，聽從家長指示走完指定的路。

遊戲後，請子女說出感受，例如：有沒有偷偷地張開眼睛？有沒有感到害怕？對家長的指示有沒有信心？

這遊戲除了訓練子女聽從指示外，還能夠培養他們信任別人，學習信靠天父。

Have the children close their eyes, no peeking, listen to an adult's instruction to walk a short distance.

After the game, ask the children how they feel. Scared? Compelled to watch? Easy to trust?

This game teaches the children how to listen to instructions and also cultivate their trust in another person, eventually putting their full faith in God.

保羅的神蹟
Paul's Miracles

使徒行傳 Acts
16:25~34, 28:1~6

掃羅後來改名叫保羅。他十分進取，四處傳福音，建立教會。

他和西拉在監裡祈禱讚美神，地震動得很厲害，牢門打開了。獄卒很害怕，但是保羅沒有乘機逃跑，反而向他們傳福音，獄卒一家都信了主。

Saul later changed his name to Paul. He traveled to places to preach and build up churches.

He and Silas were kept in prison. They loudly sang hymns to praise God. A violent earthquake shook open the prison gate. The prison guard was afraid but Paul did not take the opportunity to escape. Instead, Paul preached the good news to them. The prison guard and his family believed in the Lord.

保羅被押送到羅馬途中，有一條蛇纏住保羅，但是保羅用手把蛇扔到火裡，一點都沒有受傷。後來，保羅在羅馬放膽傳講神的國，教導主耶穌基督的事。

Paul was being sent to Rome. A snake fastened itself onto Paul, but Paul shook it off onto a fire and suffered no harm. Later on, Paul bravely preached about the Kingdom of God in Rome, teaching about the life of Jesus.

我的義人必因信得生，如果他後退，我的心就不喜悅他。

希伯來書10:38

品格塑造
進取

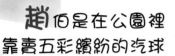

趙伯是在公園裡靠賣五彩繽紛的汽球維生的。為了吸引小朋友買汽球，他有時會放一些汽球升空。一天，一個黃皮膚的小朋友因為看見天上有紅色、黑色、白色的汽球，就沿路走到趙伯那裡。他望著那些汽球很久，就問趙伯，那個黃色的汽球是否也可以升到天上。趙伯慈祥地回答："令到汽球升空的不是外面的顏色，而是裡面的氣體。"

同樣，人要有進取的表現，不是因為外面的行為，而是裡面的態度。

禱告

親愛的主耶穌，感謝你給保羅作我的榜樣。求你加我力量，學習他的進取，即使遇見困難仍然不退後。祈禱奉耶穌的名，阿們。

207

But my righteous one shall live by faith, and if he shrinks back, my soul has no pleasure in him.

Hebrews 10:38

Character Builder
To Be Aspiring

Old Mr Chopper sells balloons in a park.

To attract as many kids as possible, he sometimes would let a few of his very colorful blimps go free in the air. One day, an Asian kid takes a long gaze at the red, black, and white flying balloons and asks Old Mr Chopper, "Does that yellow one fly, too?" The old man kindly replies, "What makes those balloons go up is not the colors outside, but the substance inside."

We can say the same about having a positive attitude – what makes one positive is hardly one's outward behavior, but inward character.

Prayer

Dear Jesus, thank you for making Paul a model. Give me strength to learn to be positive, especially as I come across many hurdles. In Your name, Amen.

想一想・做一做

1. 保羅傳福音遇過甚麼困難？但是他仍堅持下去，可見他的態度怎樣？

2. 人要有進取的表現，他先要改變的是行為，抑或是態度？

3. 至少寫下兩個方法，鍛煉你積極進取，然後在本週實踐其中一樣。

A Life Lesson

1. What hardships does Paul run into when preaching the gospel? What do we see in his character as he keeps going?

2. To cultivate an always positive attitude, do you first remodel a behavior or work on character?

3. Come up with two measures to help train a positive way of thinking. Put one into action this week.

Hoopla Whoopee Time 親手做福音天使 *DIY Angels*

童來兒嬉

神常常差派很多天使來幫助你，請帶著感恩的心，按著以下的步驟，親手做天使。

Often God sends a great many angels to help you. With a grateful heart, follow the steps below to make a DIY angel:

① 用卡紙剪出一個頭，畫上眼睛、嘴及頭髮；

② 預備一個紙杯；

③ 用紙對摺，剪出一對翅膀；

④ 用雙面膠紙將翅膀貼在紙杯背面；

⑤ 用雙面膠紙把頭貼在紙杯底部。

1　Cut out the shape of a head with cardboard paper; draw two eyes, one mouth and some hair on it.

2　Get a paper cup ready.

3　Get another piece of cardboard paper and fold it in the middle; cut out a pair of wings.

4　Glue the pair of wings to the side of the cup with double-sided adhesive tape.

5　Glue the head to the bottom of the cup with double-sided adhesive tape.

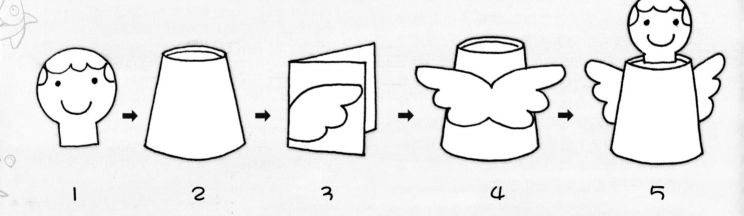

1　　2　　3　　4　　5

耶穌基督的啟示

The Revelations of Jesus Christ

啟示錄 Revelation
1:9~11, 21:1~4

使徒約翰在拔摩島上看到很多異象，那些異象都是關於耶穌基督的。神坐在天上的寶座上，眾天使和來自各族各方的人一起敬拜祂，讚美的聲音響徹天上。

The apostle John saw many visions on the island of Patmos, concerning the revelations of Jesus Christ. The Lord sat on the throne in heaven. The angels and the people from all tribes and nations worshiped Him together. The sounds of praise filled the heaven.

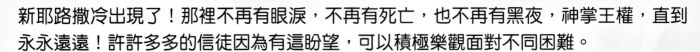

新耶路撒冷出現了！那裡不再有眼淚，不再有死亡，也不再有黑夜，神掌王權，直到永永遠遠！許許多多的信徒因為有這盼望，可以積極樂觀面對不同困難。

The New Jerusalem appeared! There will be no more tears and no more death. And there is no more night. The Lord has the authority, forever and ever. This brings hope to many believers. Jesus being the ultimate victor gives people the reason to be positive in the face of trials.

他要抹去他們的一切眼淚，不再有死亡，也不再有悲哀、哭號、痛苦，因為先前的事都過去了。

啟示錄 21:4

品格塑造
積極

Hallelujah

力克·胡哲天生沒有手腳，但是他沒有對自己和這個世界失望，反而靠著主耶穌積極生活，還帶給別人希望。他說："我是神照著祂對我的計劃所造的獨特作品。我一直努力讓自己更好，十分相信我的生命沒有限制，請想想：如果任何事都是可能的，那麼，你的人生會如何？"他沒有手腳，卻擁有別人沒有的性格，就是積極樂觀，對未來充滿盼望。

禱告

親愛的天父，感謝你為我預備天家，並藉著很多相信你的哥哥姐姐的見證鼓勵我。求你教我積極樂觀地生活。祈禱奉耶穌的名，阿們。

215

He will wipe away every tear from their eyes, and death shall be no more, neither shall there be mourning, nor crying, nor pain anymore, for the former things have passed away.

Revelation 21:4

Character Builder
To Be Positive

Nick Vujicic was born without arms and legs, but he does not despair of himself or the world. On the contrary he lives positively by relying on Jesus and brings hope to others. He says, "I am a unique creation made by God according to His plan for me. I strive to make myself better. I totally believe that my life has no limits. Think about it: if everything is possible, how would your life be?" He has no arms and legs but he has a character which others do not have: a positive optimism which is full of hope for the future.

Prayer

Dear **Father** in Heaven, thank you for preparing for me a heavenly home, and encouraging me through the witnesses of many brothers and sisters who trust in you. Teach me to live positively. In Jesus' name, Amen.

Hallelujah

想一想·做一做

1. 耶穌為人預備天家，給人甚麼盼望？

2. 為甚麼力克·胡哲雖然有缺陷，也可以充滿盼望，積極面對人生？

3. 跟家人或朋友分享力克·胡哲的見證，鼓勵他們積極生活。

A Life Lesson

1. The Lord Jesus will prepare a heavenly home for us when he comes again. How does this encourage us to live?

2. Why does Nick Vujicic have a positive outlook on life even though he faces such hardships?

3. Try to share with your family and friends the witness of Nick Vujicic to encourage them to live positively.

家長提示 Tips for Parents

積極樂觀不等於沒有憂慮，因此過分保護子女，避免他們受到挫折和失敗，有時反而令他們容易悲觀。他們遇上挫折和困難時，不妨送上鼓勵和盼望，為他們恆切祈禱，這才是恰當的做法。

Positive optimism does not mean worry-free! Being overprotective for the children, avoiding failures and defeats, may sometimes on the contrary generate pessimistic emotions. When children face difficulties and setbacks, try to give encouragement and hope. The right thing to do is to pray constantly for the children.

童來兒嬉 換個角度
Hoopla Whoopee Time *Shift a Point of View*

將以下圖畫倒轉看看，它們是否變成另一幅圖畫？

Try looking at the picture for a while. And then turn it upside down. Has it become different to you?

品格城堡
Character Castle

讀完《兒童品格聖經》後，請你在星星內寫上立志要養成的良好品格，例如：誠實、謙卑。

After reading *The CNV Kid's Bible*, write down in the stars the qualities you resolve to build the castle with, such as honesty, humbleness.

背一背
Verse
to Know

每週背一背聖經金句，背完後填上顏色作記錄。

For each verse that has been scuccessfully memorized, color its star accordingly.

1 路加福音 Luke 1:38a

2 路加福音 Luke 2:13~14

3 路加福音 Luke 2:46

4 使徒行傳 Acts 20:35b

5 約翰福音 John 4:53

6 雅各書 James 4:7a

7 哥林多前書 1 Corinthians 1:10b

8 路加福音 Luke 7:13

9 彼得前書 1 Peter 5:7

10 彼得前書 1 Peter 2:13a

11 馬可福音 Mark 6:50b

12 約翰壹書 1 John 1:9

13 馬太福音 Matthew 5:7

14 哥林多前書 1 Corinthians 13:7

15 馬太福音 Matthew 24:13

16 路加福音 Luke 17:15~16a

17 馬太福音 Matthew 26:13

18 約翰福音 John 3:16

19 羅馬書 Romans 10:11

20 使徒行傳 Acts 1:8

21 以弗所書 Ephesians 6:10

22 馬太福音 Matthew 7:9~10

23 路加福音 Luke 3:8a

24 以弗所書 Ephesians 2:8

25 希伯來書 Hebrews 10:38

26 啟示錄 Revelation 21:4